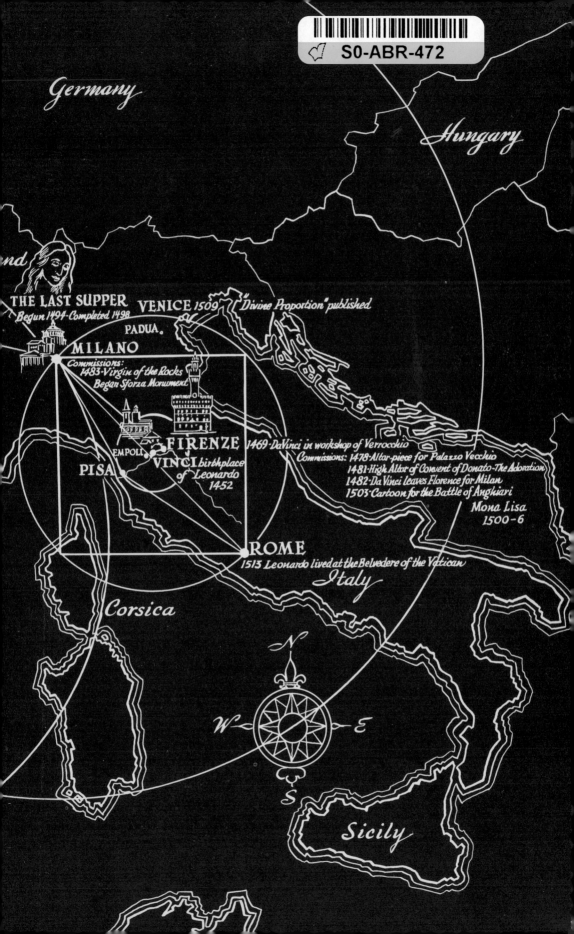

Germany

Hungary

THE LAST SUPPER
Begun 1494-Completed 1498

VENICE 1509   "Divine Proportion" published.

PADUA.

MILANO
Commissions:
1483-Virgin of the Rocks
Began Sforza Monument.

EMPOLI   FIRENZE
VINCI birthplace
PISA   of Leonardo
1452

1469-DaVinci in workshop of Verrocchio
Commissions: 1478-Altar-piece for Palazzo Vecchio
1481-High Altar of Convent of Donato-The Adoration
1482-Da Vinci leaves Florence for Milan
1503-Cartoon for the Battle of Anghiari
Mona Lisa
1500-6

ROME
1513 Leonardo lived at the Belvedere of the Vatican
Italy

Corsica

N

W   E

S

Sicily

THE LAST SUPPER
of LEONARDO DA VINCI

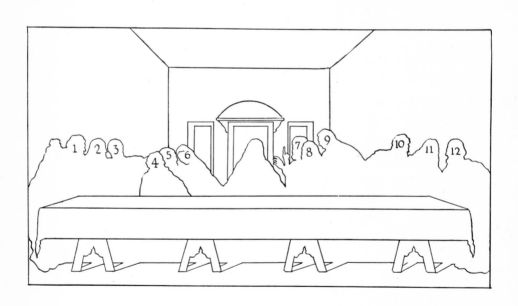

The Apostles

1. NATHANIEL BARTHOLOMEW in his astonishment has risen so quickly that his feet are still crossed as they were when he was seated.

2. JAMES THE LESS reaches behind Andrew to touch the arm of Peter, as if to ask an explanation.

3. ANDREW'S uplifted hands express horror, while his face is turned anxiously toward the Master.

4. JUDAS: between Peter and John we see the traitor Judas Iscariot vainly attempting to appear unconcerned and innocent. It is said that after the face of the Christ, the artist found that of Judas the most difficult to paint.

5. PETER is greatly excited, but feels that John is the one to ask the question, "Who is the betrayer, Lord?" In Peter's right hand he flashes a knife, ready to defend his Lord.

6. JOHN, with gentle sorrowful face, is in strong contrast with the guilty Judas.

7. THOMAS: just behind James is Thomas the honest Doubter, with one finger lifted threateningly toward the yet unknown traitor.

8. To the right of Christ, is JAMES THE GREAT, whose arms are outstretched as he looks at the Master and eagerly asks "Lord, is it I?"

9. PHILLIP, standing beside James, places his hands on his heart as he says "Thou knowest, Lord, that it is not I."

10. MATTHEW points with his arms to the Savior as if explaining to the elder disciple Simon what has just been said.

11. THADDEUS, worried and troubled, is also looking at Simon.

12. SIMON holds his hands out and looks appealingly at Christ for an explanation.

The Last Supper

of LEONARDO DA VINCI

AN ACCOUNT OF ITS RE-CREATION

BY

LUMEN MARTIN WINTER

TEXT BY

Harrison Kinney

COWARD-McCANN   NEW YORK

C O N T E N T S

ILLUSTRATIONS

THE LAST SUPPER
of LEONARDO DA VINCI

C H A P T E R   I

The Commission

ONE MORNING in April, 1951, a man stood before the entrance to 96 Fifth Avenue in New York City, checking the address against a newspaper clipping he held in his hand. The building was the former Martin Van Buren mansion that had long since been converted into business offices and art studios. The man stepped inside the tiny lobby and approached the elevator operator.

"I'm looking for the studio of the artist, Lumen Martin Winter," said the stranger, speaking in a southern accent. "Is this the right address?"

It was the right address. In his large, sky-lighted studio Lumen Martin Winter was working on a water-color of a desert scene in the American southwest. He was a prematurely gray-headed man in his early forties with a young face, a soft manner of speaking and a sincere enthusiasm for his vocation.

Winter's father had been a construction engineer whose occupation kept him and his family in a state of constant migration. Lumen was born in Ellerie, Illinois; a town difficult to locate on most maps. When Lumen was three his father settled in Belpre,

3

Kansas, and then in Aberdeen, Ohio. The youngster's flair for drawing was quickly evident and by the time he was thirteen his illustrations were being produced in the *American Boy*. His father's occupational pursuits finally took the Winter family to Grand Rapids, Michigan. It was there, while Lumen was attending high school, that the youngster became first a part-time and then a fully employed editorial cartoonist for the late Arthur Vandenburg, publisher of the *Grand Rapids Herald*.

A newspaper cartoonist is never quite sure if he is an artist or a pictorial journalist and Winter wanted beyond any doubt to be an artist. When he had completed two years of junior college in Grand Rapids he pushed on to Cleveland, where he began his formal study of art. All ambitious and hopeful American artists plan against the day when they feel strong and sure enough to lay siege to the nation's center of fine arts, New York City. New York is generous with the successful artist, but only sympathetic to the untried. Winter took a job in that city drawing advertising posters by day and attended the National Academy of Design at night. Gradually his career acquired momentum. By the time he was seeking further professional improvement at the Grand Central School of Art, his illustrations were being used regularly as the covers of *Liberty* magazine, which in the early nineteen-thirties was riding a high crest of public acceptance.

There came a day when an art instructor told Winter, "You have a painter's point of view toward art and life; certainly not an illustrator's." It was what Winter had been waiting to hear.

Mural painting had always appealed to Lumen Winter. He saw no reason why sensitive craftsmanship should be confined to small canvases. He liked the great reaches of landscape that are

4

possible in a mural, and the expressive giants who people them. He eagerly accepted the chance to assist Ezra Winter (no relation) in painting the *Search for the Fountain of Youth* theme on the wall of the grand foyer of the new Rockefeller Center Music Hall. When the job was completed, Lumen knew, and his colleagues knew, that he was going to be a mural artist.

The times were still the gaunt years of the great depression, the years of competing with other mural artists for the few chances to brush their murals on the walls of municipal buildings, post-offices, private clubs or public memorial edifices. Winter won all the work he could handle. He was describing his style of painting, by then, as modern and semi-abstract, but it also showed a comfortable knowledge of the academic. His art exhibits began to attract public attention and favorable criticism, and at the time that this story began Winter had become recognized as one of the country's better mural artists.

"Are you Lumen Martin Winter?" asked the man in the doorway. The man, of middle age, was dressed casually in shirt sleeves and a wide-brimmed hat. He waited for Winter's hesitant affirmation. "I'm Eugene Holton," he continued then. "I live in Biscayne Key, Miami Beach. I saw a picture in yesterday's afternoon paper of a large mural you just did for the Brooklyn Savings Bank. Well, I came up here to New York to find a mural artist who can do things like that. I hope what I have to say will interest you."

Holton had seen a pictorial essay in a weekly magazine a short time before, he told Winter, that told the tragic story of how Leonardo da Vinci's celebrated painting of the *Last Supper* was rapidly decaying on its wall in the old monastery dining-room,

5

now a museum in Milan. "I was so bothered by the thought of it," Holton went on, "that I couldn't eat or sleep properly for three days and nights. A week ago I had a frightening dream about it that awakened me in the middle of the night. It may sound incredible to you but I decided right then that I would be troubled the rest of my life if I didn't find some artist who would duplicate da Vinci's *Last Supper* for me. Not just another copy of it, you understand, but a replica, I suppose you'd call it; the same size and, as nearly as possible, the same picture that da Vinci first painted. I'd pay an artist to go abroad and study it."

Winter sat in stunned amazement while Holton talked on. He had been in the real estate business, he said, in both North and South Carolina and was willing now to invest a good part of his savings in commissioning the project that had become an obsession with him. He planned, furthermore, to build a chapel of the exact dimensions of the room that housed the original classic and to hang there the finished reproduction, or replica, for art lovers, art historians and all Christianity to see and to glory in. "My wife told me," Holton added, "that if I don't go through with it I'll be unhappy the rest of my life."

The proposal struck Winter as something of a heady brew. Emotionally it impressed him immediately as irresistible. To be given the chance to prolong the life, or the approximate life, of a renowned masterpiece with its artistic ingeniousness and its religious significance should be considered, Winter realized, a privilege and a worthy challenge. On the other hand, would attempting the task earn him doubtful fame as a copyist and jeopardize his reputation as an authentic, original person? How did one measure the degrees of artistic pretentiousness or reverent dedication in such a matter, and which quality would finally dominate? Where

6

Interior of the New York Studio

7

did honest endeavor at recreating in the name of Leonardo end, and commercial plagiarism begin?

Rationalizing doubts is a simple process for a man who feels himself touched by destiny. And Winter felt touched by destiny. Few artists completely survive their early dreams of matching in some way the classical works of the old masters. Winter's first earnings as a teen-age artist had been spent in purchasing the volumes of da Vinci's notebooks. The universality of Leonardo's genius still made those writings the text for modern art lessons on such subjects as anatomy, the inter-play of light and shade and the three-dimensional quality of painting known as perspective. The man was not simply an historical oddity. His designs for airplanes and instruments of warfare, his scientific prophecies, all conceived years before their eventual realization, kept his memory and record important living testaments to the evolution of Western man's civilization. Winter could not approach the task as merely a technical commission to fulfill. Da Vinci's constant inquiries into the nature of things had seemed to bring God into a better focus for him. Religion and art and science were frequently inseparable for da Vinci and one could not, in studying his work, dissociate the one from the others. Repainting the *Last Supper* would be more an adventure of the spirit, Winter believed, than just a highly aesthetic satisfaction.

"I don't see how I can refuse," he told Holton after a half hour of floor-pacing and deliberation. "I shall ask only enough payment from you to cover my expenses. I'll chalk it off as a traveling fellowship."

When a man seeks to hunt down, to catch and hold and then to emulate the creative productions of another's mind, he walks a tightrope indeed. And when Winter undertook the repainting of da Vinci's masterpiece, he had to proceed on the assumption that he was a thousand times removed from the original experience. He had to allow for the elements of the centuries which have progressively concealed clues as to what has gone on before. He had to recognize and clear away the interfering work of others who once sought to restore the painting six times over and in the end only hastened its rate of ruin. What troubled Winter down to the day of his own re-creation's unveiling was: could he accurately transmit the vital spiritual proclamation that is still so accessible in da Vinci's crumbling masterpiece?

Winter's best insurance against failure, as it turned out, was his intelligent awareness that all mystical intangibles which impel an artist to greatness can never be forcibly re-experienced. They can come to one who waits in sensitive, obedient humility.

That evening Winter made out what he termed "A Statement of Intention" to serve as his credo throughout the course of the project. "I shall do all the detective work and study possible," he wrote, "in the attempt to relive or to understand all those environmental factors and everyday experiences that added up to the person of Leonardo. I realize that my impressions will not always rise above my own background and that my approach will have been conditioned by elements that have nothing in common with Leonardo. But I shall hope that in the final analysis my sincere intentions and my spiritual consciousness of the mission will reward me with just enough of whatever universal enlightenment blessed Leonardo to permit a faithful rendering of his *Last Supper*. A picture's technique and composition, I realize, may be learned and copied, but a picture's message is the important part of it and the most difficult to transmit. My aim will be to keep faith with Leonardo insofar as I know how, for then I cannot betray myself."

9

Castello Vinci

10

The Man from Vinci

NO MAN CAN say whether the candle flame of genius, which was Leonardo's, needed the pure oxygen of the Italian Renaissance to flame as brightly as it did. No one knows whether in a period of less intellectual inquiry he would have applied his remarkable inventive talents to any extent. He was, at any rate, born at a good time. The year was 1452. The Hundred-Years War between France and England had just come to a close and the following year Constantinople would fall to the Turks, marking the official end of the age of empire. Although the transition is scarcely noticeable, except in retrospect, one era cannot perish without giving birth to another. The new age in Italy was the Renaissance.

Italy in the fourteenth century had been first to stir from the paralysis that gripped most of western civilization during the Middle Ages. The country was composed of many small states, each ruled by a prince, jealous of the others. The Roman Church, which had contributed the only unifying element to the country's political structure, was in a state of decay. The people who began with a criticism of hedonistic Popes and corrupt clergy were soon questioning the very dogma of the Church which had taught them that worldly life was not worth the energy of evaluation, but was a drab antechamber to the hereafter—the real reward.

But self-negation has never been an enduring characteristic of humans, and the Italians happily welcomed a rebirth of old ideas; ideas that granted a man his right as an individual to be different, and to ask questions about himself and the universe; ideas that freed the race from perpetual Purgatory and set it in pursuit of knowledge, color and beauty with which to enlighten the mind and warm the soul. The hunger for loveliness motivated a host of talented writers, poets, sculptors, musicians and artists into a frenzy of inspired activity.

By the time of Leonardo's birth, the study of ancient Latin and Greek writers was the ardent occupation of all who pretended to scholasticism. The study became known as Humanism. Petrarch, Boccaccio and Cyriac of Ancona offered the teachings of pre-Christian philosophers as evidence of man's rationality and dignity. The extremists—and there are always a few among converts —followed their excited emotions into an acceptance of paganism and atheism. But the large majority of Renaissance scholars and art practitioners inevitably recognized a larger mystery beyond every philosophical conception, beyond every natural phenomenon explained and beyond every result of artistic creation. Many of the Renaissance clergy were still profligate, but the churches and cathedrals were increasingly aglow with great art that spoke articulately and lastingly for the religious mindedness of the period.

The tiny village of Vinci, birthplace of Leonardo, still lives on among the Tuscan hills. The river Arno passes near Vinci, and up the valley twenty miles away is Florence. Villages in Leonardo's day looked to the nearby city for its trade and protection, and in 1452 Vinci was in the Florentine orbit. It was an age when individualism could not be expressed politically and Florence's one hundred thousand people were under the benevolent dictatorship of the Medici, the house which would one day sponsor Leonardo.

Leonardo was born April 15, five hundred and one years ago. He was the illegitimate son of Ser Piero, a notary public, and of a peasant girl. Ser Piero, subsequently disappointed at having no children by the woman his family insisted he marry, claimed Leonardo as his own. The child was an inveterate observer of nature from the moment his faculties of investigation were at all developed. He sketched impressions of peculiar rocks and strange plants, or unusual animals that engaged his imagination while he was exploring the Tuscan countryside. He had no time for the commonplace, in nature or (later) art.

Ser Piero, coming across his young son's sketches, proposed that he paint whatever he wished on a wooden panel for him. Young Leonardo, displaying a bizarre turn of mind, created a fantastic flame-belching monster. The work startled his father, but the man recognized ability when he saw it and sold the panel in Florence for ten ducats. It was not long after that that Ser Piero, who had influential friends in Florence, arranged for Leonardo to begin study there under Andrea del Verrocchio.

The year was 1472. Florence, for all that its rule was dictated by the brothers Guiliano and Lorenzo de' Medici, was proving itself the first modern state of the world. A new upper-class of citizens had become wealthy through commerce and industry and, most conspicuously, through lending money at breath-taking rates of interest. With the power that goes with money, Florence exerted a mighty influence over foreign governments in both the Christian and Moslem worlds. The Italian language was being fostered (obtaining a good start in Dante's *Inferno*) and patriotism was becoming a factor in international dealings. Political science, which Machiavelli would soon refine to a skilled and shrewd game, was, as yet, mainly intrigue, usurpation of power by despots, and surprise wars.

The wealth of Florence made the city an easy market for fine arts. There were forty-four goldsmiths on the Ponte Vecchio, near which Verrocchio's own goldsmith's shop and studio were located. Splendid products included arabesques sculptured out of marble and sandstone, wood-carving, silver and gold embroidery, jewelry and portraits.

Verrocchio, Leonardo's teacher, was a goldsmith, sculptor and artist. For that day was not one of specialization. A man with an artistic flair in one field felt obligated to achieve a competence in another. The period was universal when all things were possible and no horizon couldn't be overtaken. "Men can do all things, if they will," said Leon Battista Alberti, a Florentine architect who died in the year that Leonardo came to Florence. The coveted reputation was one for versatility, not perfection in any one thing. Only rarely, as in the case of Leonardo, is man privileged to stretch out his hand and touch the soul of the universe, the fountain of *all* discovery, understanding and expression.

The first work believed to be Leonardo's that is still in existence is an angel which he painted on one of Verrocchio's altar decora-

Ponte Vecchio

tions. Except for a few portraits, the finest art of the day was being performed for churches, either under the sponsorship of the clergy or of the ruling noblemen who preferred to celebrate their piety conspicuously. Unhappily for posterity, it was to be significant that Leonardo's first recognizable painting made up only a fragment of the picture. For with the universe speaking to him, Leonardo could not long persist at any one task. His record as we know it today is a glorious collection of fragments; glimpses of genius in art, sculpturing, architecture, engineering, anatomy, and the natural sciences. To him it made little difference whether he was painting a Madonna or discovering fossils on a rocky hillside. Science and art were one, for da Vinci, and he no doubt regarded his life at its end as having been a unified whole, however piecemeal it might seem to others.

As an artist he would habitually spend so much time preparing sketches for a projected painting that, once having solved the architectural problems of the work, he lost interest in its execution. A very few of his paintings that are still with us show that

15

he quickly turned over the task of completing a job to his assistants. Giorgio Vasari, an Italian biographer (1511-1574) wrote of Leonardo: "He began many things, then left them unfinished."

Before he left Verrocchio's employ Leonardo had become obsessed with mathematics, which for awhile he believed to be the only perfect science. A hungry mind that had to feed upon so mixed a diet could make no ready impression in Florence. Florence, which in that day has been commonly described as the most important workshop of Italy and of the modern European spirit, attracted to it the greatest workmen. But to earn the favor of the Medici one had also to be productive in one's work, and Leonardo could seldom sustain interest in a project to see it through to its completion. Weary of the nagging demands of clergymen for work promised them, da Vinci accepted Lorenzo's sponsorship as an emissary to the court of Milan. He left behind two uncompleted altar pieces: *St. Jerome* and the *Adoration of the Magi*.

The year was 1482 and Leonardo was thirty. He entered Milan as a court musician, having made with his hands a silver lyre which he played to Lorenzo's great satisfaction. But there was little honor in being recommended to the Duke of Milan as minstrel, for Lorenzo, it was widely known, jealously hoarded all Florentine artists whom he regarded highly. Leonardo had not produced enough to merit recognition.

The ruler of Milan was a despot named Lodovico, Il Moro. It was an age of despotism. Ruling dynasties were continually being formed on illegitimate claims and seizures, only to be overthrown in turn by conspiring kinsmen. The Sforza family had ruled Milan since 1447 when Francesco Sforza, a soldier of fortune, had taken over as absolute monarch. Many self-made rulers had begun as

16

mercenary generals in the employ of princes and had then become dangerously ambitious when success in battle made them popular with their army and the people at home. The higher type of soldier-adventurer, known as a *condotteri,* invariably dreamed of founding his own dynasty. Sforza realized the dream. His son, Galeazzo Maria, who succeeded him, managed to carry on for ten years before he was murdered in 1476. The murdered man's son, the heir-designate, was thrown into prison by his uncle, Lodovico, who usurped power and had been living in the Citadel of Milan as titular head for six years when Leonardo joined his court.

This was part of the usual pattern. A usurper at best sat uncomfortably on his throne. In addition to his bodyguard of mercenaries, a tyrant collected people of talent around him mainly to celebrate his name and cement the permanency of his rule in the eyes of the public and rival states. The most honorable alliance an illegitimate ruler could make, as one historian wrote referring to those times, was with intellectual merit. Such a man hungered after fame and nursed a passion for monuments or flattery. Unfortunately for the performing men of (as yet) little-known talent, like Leonardo, only a few favorites were given regular financial support. But Leonardo's adaptable mind was quite up to the challenge.

A tyrant who had dispossessed a kinsman had to proceed on the assumption that there was constant intrigue against himself, unfriendly alliances menacing his tenure of rule, and that eventually there could well be a show-down on the battlefield. So at last Lodovico listened to Leonardo when he represented himself as a military engineer. Leonardo described to his patron by illustrated letter, his new inventions for battering down city walls, or repelling attackers. He thought up a conical-shaped armored wagon and a chariot equipped with long scythes intended to cut the legs off enemy troops. Gunpowder had been only recently invented, but Leonardo conceived of a breach-loading gun. This man, whose life record would be buried for decades, worked out the details of a pre-fabricated bridge that could be quickly erected for the crossing of rivers by troops and quickly disassembled after the passage.

The display of mechanical ingenuity by Leonardo soon earned him the role of master of Lodovico's court pageants. There was ever the need, for a ruler of shaky claim, to dazzle the public with pompous displays of costumed processions, pantomimes in the public square and city-wide celebrations at royal marriages that were frequently arranged to improve the relations between two rival states. The pageant themes invariably shouted the glories of the tyrant to high heaven, claiming, by metaphor and symbol, his popularity and excellence as a ruler. Within the palace walls, the court pageants tended to be more theatrical but none the less flattering.

Leonardo won Lodovico's wholehearted favor after several court festivities in which Leonardo had painted the backdrops (they frequently depicted planets and stars) for the spectacles and rigged mechanical contraptions that amazed the ducal audiences. At one palace show, Leonardo made a papier-mâché lion that stalked onto the stage, advanced toward Lodovico and then exploded into paper flowers. There had to be a favorable point of course. The lion symbolized Lodovico as a stout-hearted duke and the flowers paid tribute to his accomplishments in the more genteel aspects of living.

18

The man from Vinci had been over a year in Milan when he was granted a commission to do an altar piece by the fraternity of the Immaculate Conception. The commission's fulfillment was slow and not to the monks' liking. Although posterity would one day consider the *Madonna of the Rocks* one of the art world's finest possessions, a quarrel over the terms of payment on Leonardo's part began, not to be settled until years later when Leonardo would paint a replica of the work, this time leaving most of the labor to assistants.

The times were one of condoned immorality, and it was quite in order for Lodovico to request one of his court artists to paint the portrait of his mistress, Cecilia Gallerani. Leonardo's *Lady with the Ermine* is that seventeen-year-old girl, painted with the tender attention the Florentine gave all his women subjects, be they the Virgin Mary or a woman of doubtful reputation.

Milan, whose cultural accomplishments lagged considerably behind those of Florence, Venice and Rome, could at least boast the splendid cathedral engineered by Giangaliazzo in 1385. The dome had never been completed and Lodovico invited several leading architects to submit plans and estimates for finishing the building. Leonardo's sketch of his ideas for the cathedral is still preserved and pronounced today as aesthetically and architecturally sound, but he did not win the assignment. Da Vinci would not leave architectural or sculptured monuments to his memory (as would Michelangelo), and only a precious few paintings. But his prophetic omniscience would be recorded in his notebooks and his memorials would one day be evident everywhere in the ways of modern life.

The plague of the Black Death swept Milan during the winter

of 1485-1486. Leonardo correctly attributed the cause to the lack of sanitation in the city. He drew up plans for Lodovico, recommending a widening of the streets, a sewerage system and means of preventing the polluting of drinking water. So great a civic task would mean money, and Lodovico's life of luxury was already dangerously dependent on high taxes. One citizen had already had to be strangled for complaining against the duke's levies. The plan was forgotten and the plague eventually ran its course.

Lodovico was not popular with the Milanese and an unpopular dictator knows that his political enemies can recruit powerful opposition against him. He decided to remind the people of the greatness Milan had reached under the Sforza family. Sculptors were invited to submit bids for an equestrian statue of the General, Francesco Sforza, father of Lodovico. The General had been a brave, respected and loved man, carried on the shoulders of his people and even loaned money by bankers of states at war with him at the time.

Leonardo would not lose out again in competitive bidding. His design for the rearing horse and heroic rider was not only daring in size beyond all those of his rivals, but it would require two hundred thousand pounds of bronze to be cast. The famous sculptors were skeptical of the proportions. They could not see how such a top-heavy arrangement could support itself, but Lodovico's vanity was involved. His father's statue must be the biggest. The grant went to Leonardo.

Da Vinci began work on the giant horse and rider in 1489 but when he was nearing completion of the clay model three years later, he became dissatisfied with the form and balance of his creation and destroyed it. A second model, twenty-three feet high,

Leonardo's Study for the Head of Christ

21

was eventually completed and was placed on public display in the castle courtyard. The court and public were dumbfounded with wonder at the towering sculpture, and Leonardo's fame was finally secured in his own day.

It didn't matter to da Vinci that the statue could not be cast and that the clay model would soon crumble. His joy had been in its creation and the solving of a hundred thousand laws of physics and mathematics. The days were ones of trouble, of quick, unpredictable wars, and the bronze for the statue's casting was needed for artillery. "Of the horse I will say nothing," he wrote Lodovico with characteristic forbearance, when he learned that the monument could not be cast, "because I know the times." The huge clay statue would soon be used as a target for archers among French occupational troops.

The Church of Santa Maria delle Grazie was conveniently situated near the Duke's castle. Lodovico frequently walked the monastery garden, worshipped within the chapel, received special guests within its secluded walls or there gave himself up to solitary reflections. Alterations were needed within the church and Lodovico, who was appreciative of the monks and regarded the establishment with something of an air of ownership, assumed the responsibilities for the expense and directions of the repairing and decorating. The bare walls of the brothers' dining-room, or refectory, were to be adorned with religious murals. Montorfano painted a fresco, the *Crucifixion,* on the rear wall, completing it in 1495. Leonardo, by now Lodovico's favorite, was awarded the wall facing it.

His choice of subject was an obvious one. A refectory wall in a monastery suggested at once the famous last supper of Christ and

Crucifixion *by Montorfano*

His disciples. Leonardo began work on the *Last Supper* in 1494. It was apparent to those who knew him and his habits that this painting was to be something out of the ordinary. There were not the long intervals of inattention that had been typical of Leonardo in his other commissions. He had never before concentrated his artistic, manual and spiritual powers to such a supreme degree, and he would not again. The mighty task required four years, and when it was completed, all Italy and the kings of other countries knew of Leonardo, the man from the Tuscan hills. It was as though Leonardo regarded his masterpiece throughout its creation as a partial payment to God for the divine gift of mortal genius. For Leonardo knew well that no man is ordained to possess universal insight only to hoard the knowledge; a man who catches fire from the sparks of a cosmic awareness, must kindle other fires or be consumed himself. The *Last Supper* was Leonardo's spiritual acknowledgment of indebtedness. There could be no postponement of labor where it was concerned; no bickering over the material terms of payment. Within Leonardo's lifetime, the great mural began to crack and peel to the chagrin and despair of all art lovers of the high Renaissance. But Leonardo accepted the fact quietly.

The generations to come would ponder over the mysticism in the fading *Last Supper* and the mystery about the *Mona Lisa*. The secret between Leonardo and the universe was evident in all his work, and if it was not always readily understandable to others, that was of little concern to Leonardo.

The famous mural was scarcely dry on its wall when the political fortunes of its sponsor, the Duke of Milan, Lodovico, took a turn for the worse. Franco Sacchetti wrote once: "As despotisms rise, grow, and are consolidated, so grows in their midst the hidden element which must produce their dissolution and ruin." Lodovico, whose vanity had led him at one point to remark that the Pope was his personal chaplain, and the French King his courier, was faced now by a powerful alliance of enemies: hostile Italian dukedoms and Charles VIII of France. He fled to Switzerland before invading armies, to return the next year with a force of mercenaries. For a few weeks more he was again ruler of Milan and then his most trusted *condottiere* went over to the enemy and Lodovico was taken to France a prisoner. He died in a castle dungeon several years later, having written on the wall of his cell in French: "I am unhappy."

Leonardo was left deprived of his patron in a city occupied by foreign troops. He was in no physical danger, of course. Men of science and of the arts were immune from the fickle interplay of the times, much more so than after the emergence of militant nationalism. Leonardo would soon serve as military engineer to the Florentines in their campaign against Pisa and next serve as adviser to the French King in a war against Florence. The important thing to him was that he be allowed to apply his ideas, to enter his thoughts in his expanding notebooks and find a patron who would allow him the leisure for his important experiments. Leonardo knew the times, and he was not particular about a benefactor's moral allegiances, or the purposes of a war that was being waged. He accepted what he had to in order to get on with his work and his dreams.

Venice, still a powerful and wealthy commercial port in 1500, was being challenged by the Turks who were edging their aggressive way nearer and nearer. Turkish ships were sailing dangerously close to Venetian waters. Leonardo arrived in the city in March of that year. His offer of service as military adviser for the defense of Venice was hurriedly accepted. His plans were multiple. They utilized rivers and similar natural obstacles to invading warriors. He enthusiastically submitted a sketch for a submarine-type craft capable of sinking enemy vessels by surprise. But he was still ahead of his times. The ideas impressed the Venetians as too far-fetched. At that, they might have tried them out as

25

last, desperate measures, but the Turkish threat subsided and Leonardo's conceptions of naval warfare were put aside for another three hundred years.

After sixteen years away, Leonardo returned to Florence. Verrocchio was dead; the Medici temporarily exiled. But Leonardo's fame had preceded him there and made a place for him. He was now the man whose giant equestrian monument in Milan was the wonder of sculptors and whose *Last Supper* was drawing crowds to the Church of the Santa Maria delle Grazie, crowds that frequently included the French governor. The handsome golden hair was graying now, and his comely, sensitive features were becoming angular with the years, his tall frame a little bent.

Leonardo was pressed to do an altar piece for the Church of the Annunciation in Florence. He chose to depict the Virgin Mary seated in the lap of Saint Anne, a somewhat astonishing arrangement to be injected into the tradition of religious painting. The preliminary cartoon for the work was completed about Easter, 1501, and the delighted Servite monks allowed the curious Florentines to parade for two days through Leonardo's room in the monastery to view the result. But the problems of geometry, balance, perspective, shade and light had been resolved in the drawing of the cartoon. Transferring the cartoon to the altar piece as a finished work was anti-climactic for Leonardo. He lost interest in the commission and for the next several months became immersed in studies of geometry.

A new despot had appeared upon the scene. He was Cesare Borgia, Duke of Valentinois and son of Pope Alexander VI, the first Pope to publicly recognize his children. Cesare seemed incapable of a decent thought or act. He had stolen his territories, and notable people, who might one day be his enemies, had been poisoned or stabbed to death while visiting as trusting guests in his palace. His body was gripped by a ghastly disease that was soon to end his life, and the infection seemed to have spread to his very soul. In a day of intrigue, treason and political murder, when constant danger made tyrants of most absolute rulers, Cesare was held in contempt by rival dictators. But greater than their contempt was their fear of his power and clever strategy which so often seem to favor the godless.

Cesare for a time had found it expedient to use the King of France as his ally, and he was mightily impressed when he learned that Louis XII, upon discovering the *Last Supper* after his arrival in Milan, was so enraptured by the mural that he had demanded it be moved to France even though it mean dismantling the building. (He had changed his mind, fearing the picture's destruction.) To give his regime a badly needed prestige in the eyes of the French monarch, therefore, Cesare requested the services of Leonardo, author of the painting, as military engineer. The Florentine, now fifty years old, was glad to get away from the nagging monks of Florence who were demanding that he complete his painting of the *Virgin and Saint Anne.*

This period of service in the employ of Italy's most spectacular villain was a fruitful one for Leonardo. His notebooks brimmed with the findings of his relentless and curious investigations. He found fossil relics imbedded in the rocks of mountain sides and was staggered by the ancient age he knew the earth must be. He stood transfixed by the seashore and watched the characteristics of the pounding breakers, and discerned a cosmic rhythm that he guessed to be the heartbeat of the universe. He knew to a surprising degree of accuracy the cause of rain and its physical properties, the composition of earth and the growth of plants. In a day when a host of people were wrestling with the new proposition that the earth was a globe, Leonardo had long persuaded himself that our earthly planet revolves around the sun.

Not all theses upon which he compiled scientific findings had been intuitively acquired; he was versed in Aristotle and all the ancients whom the Humanists were still quoting and discussing. He had no arbitrary theory as to what life and the world were; he did not waste his energy in bending every discovery and observation to fit a "logical system." He cheerfully accepted the mysteries that have always been withheld from mortals, and enjoyed his privilege as a man of the universe to examine and wonder at them. Keeping his mind open and receptive, he collected fragments of truths that would one day be used in times of more organized investigation to advance his theories.

Meanwhile, he was serving Cesare in a practical capacity. In Peombino he submitted plans for the erection of new buildings, the draining of marshes and the subsequent reclamation of flooded land. As "architect and engineer-in-chief," the man from Vinci traveled to Siena, Arezzo, Urbino, and Rimini. In Pesaro he spent long and contented hours in the library established by Alessandro Sforza, reading cosmographic, astrological and medical books. For by now he was interested in the stars and planets of the night sky, which he called in his notes, "the vault of heaven." But his reports to his employer were faithfully rendered. A canal should be constructed, insisted Leonardo, between Cesena and the port of Cesanatico. And so it was, but by engineers of a later day.

In 1503 Leonardo was back in Florence. He was now filling

Leonardo's drawing called Destruction Reigning from Heaven
having a decided resemblance of an atomic explosion

Leonardo at work

the pages of his journal with sketches and ideas about the theory of bird-flight which he felt man could one day emulate. He purchased caged pigeons in the public square and released them, watching them carefully as the birds ascended in flight, soared and circled. He was soon constructing an airplane with wings designed like a bird's. In all probability he put the completed flying machine to a test which was not successful because the subject was dropped forever from his notebooks after a certain date. The pain of failure would have been considerable. The laws of

30

physics, which he knew and believed in, had misled him at some point of reckoning and Leonardo regarded such error as his own betrayal of nature's trust.

Florence was soon at war with Pisa. Leonardo, still agile at adapting himself to any change of political conditions, offered an engineering plan to the Florentines that was accepted. Pisa, situated on the Arno a few miles inland from the sea, depended on the river for its trade and communication. Leonardo proposed to change the course of the river above Pisa and channel the water into the sea at Leghorn, leaving Pisa landlocked. Leonardo spent several months in the camp of the Florentine army above Pisa, supervising the herculean task of digging two canals to carry the water of the Arno to Leghorn. Peace was made between the two cities before the project was far along, and the people of Pisa joyfully filled in the partially dug ditches. Leonardo was accustomed to uncompleted plans. He immediately submitted a peacetime plan for constructing a commercial canal between the now friendly peoples of Florence and Pisa. The river was not navigable its entire length and the obstacles of dredging seemed too considerable to two communities weary from recent fighting. This plan, too, with its blueprints for locks enabling vessels to be carried by water over ridges and shallows, was set aside.

During his youth in Florence, Leonardo had described painting as mankind's noblest calling. He remained, first and last, a painter. "The painter," he wrote, "is lord of all types of people and all things." It was not difficult for the city of Florence to persuade Leonardo to undertake the decoration of the council chamber in the Palazzo della Signoria. He was requested to select, for painting, phases of the Florentine victory over Milan at Anghiari bridge,

31

sixty-three years before. Weary at last of creating tranquil Madonnas, Leonardo chose to picture as the first scene the stormy crisis of the battle, crowded with rearing horses, fallen knights and the glittering lances and swords of those who fought on for possession of the Milanese standard. Among the sketches of Leonardo's notebooks are figures of the horses he loved to draw; horses penciled with a thorough knowledge of all their anatomical peculiarities and exquisite in their nobleness of form. The early horse sketches were made by Leonardo in preparation for the Sforza equestrian monument but the later drawings were Leonardo's conscientious searchings for animals worthy of the Anghiari mural.

A master-planner, Leonardo was seldom inclined to begin a mural by painting directly on the wall. In this case he embodied the sketches of his groundwork in a giant cartoon of the battle scene, intending to transfer it upon completion to the chamber wall. The wall was (and is) fifty yards long by ten yards high, and the cartoon may have been scaled to size. News of the great pasteboard painting taking place in the Sala del Papa at Santa Maria Novella was soon abroad but it was not this alone that brought excited art students and practitioners from all over Italy to Florence. A fantastically dramatic situation had arisen. In a big room at the dyers' hospital of Sant' Onofrio, Michelangelo, whose mighty marble statue of David had just been unveiled in the Loggia dei Lanzi, was at work on a cartoon destined for the wall in the council chamber opposite Leonardo's.

The rivalry was bitterly hostile as far as the temperamental Michelangelo was concerned. Leonardo was dumbfounded as to why this should be so but he could not remain indifferent to the challenge. He had made a sketch of Michelangelo's *David* as he made sketches of everything that interested him. Perhaps the hypersensitive Michelangelo had resented Leonardo's public suggestion that *David* be erected in the Loggia lest it interfere with festivities in the Uffizi palace, a previously recommended site for the statue. Whatever the reason, the young sculptor, upon meeting Leonardo one day in the Piazza della Trinita, suddenly exploded in wrath. He taunted the gentle man from Vinci for the failure to cast the equestrian statue at Milan. "And those fat geese of Milan," he added, "trusted such a task to you!" Leonardo made no mention of the incident in his notebooks. If he suspected that Michelangelo suffered from a sense of persecution he chose forbearance in the face of its evidence. "Increase your patience in the face of great wrongs and they will then be powerless to vex your mind," he reminded himself in his journal.

The very sight of Leonardo, meticulously dressed and groomed, still splendidly handsome at fifty-two, seemed to upset Michelangelo. The young man, with his broken nose, homely features, body, hair and clothes never clean of marble dust, believed that even the time required to dress carefully should be spent in artistic creation. No doubt he felt, too, that a man of Leonardo's pretensions was unfaithful to his calling by expending his energies in intellectual pursuits far afield from painting and sculpture. Or perhaps he was envious of a mind constantly engaged in diversified subjects that kept Leonardo at peace with himself, a truce that Michelangelo would never bring about. At any rate he demanded that the city councilors permit *him* a wall of the council chamber to paint. The entire chamber had been promised to Leonardo, of course, and Michelangelo had done only a little painting, but this was the man who had sculptured *David,* and Leonardo's reputation as a slow and unreliable worker was not overlooked. In October, 1504, Michelangelo was awarded the wall opposite that reserved for Leonardo. The paradox of Leonardo, creator of gentle Virgins and placid landscapes, portraying the violence of war was now increased by the subject chosen by Michelangelo, molder of the furious *Battle of Hercules and the Centaurs:* the Florentine soldiers bathing in the river at Anghiari just at the moment when the enemy came upon them.

Among those who journeyed to Florence to witness this battle of skill between titans was Raphael. He was then twenty-one, a native of Urbino and student of Pietro Perugino. Michelangelo would one day influence Raphael with his biblical paintings on the ceiling of the Sistine Chapel in Rome but at this stage of the youngster's career, his heart and hopes reached out toward Leonardo's amazing art. "When he saw the work of Leonardo," wrote Vasari, speaking of Raphael, "he set himself to study it with the utmost zeal, for it pleased him more than anything he had ever seen. But whatever he did, and in spite of his best endeavor, he could not surpass that master."

Leonardo and Michelangelo worked separately on their scaffolding for two years. Pope Julius II, who wished his tomb built by the young creator of *David,* persuaded Michelangelo to leave his work in Florence for a time. In the midst of this imposing task at Rome, Michelangelo, with typical lack of control, fancied himself slighted by the Pope upon one trivial occasion and returned to Florence and the completing of the Anghiari mural. And Leonardo strayed from *his* commitments, as usual. He had begun painting the portrait of the Mona Lisa and was occasionally penciling sketches for the picture that would one day be his *Leda and the Swan*. Still, work on the mural went on, and by 1506 Leonardo and his helpers had transferred the "Fight for the Flag" to the wall of the Great Hall of the Council. The mural was to have been made up of three panels, the battle for the flag making up the center section.

But Leonardo's life was destined to be lived out among wrecked dreams and unrealized plans. Impatient with the battle picture's damp, fresh colors that were slow to dry on the plaster, Leonardo built a fire near the wall to more quickly solidify the oils. Unfortunately he had used an adhesive agent of his own invention in the paints and to the horror of the spectators, the waves of heat started streams of bright colors running down the new mural, colors that collided and merged into a galaxy of ruin. Leonardo could not bring himself to begin again. What his *Battle of Anghiari* must have been like we know only because of the pitifully few sketches relating to it and especially because of Peter Paul Rubens, who nearly a century later was touring Italy as an art student and came upon the da Vinci cartoon in Florence. Feeling the necessity of preserving a great vanishing art by re-creating it again in a more lasting form—a compulsion that would overtake an American artist three hundred and fifty years afterward—Rubens copied the "Fight for the Flag" in chalk and shaded it in sepia. Leonardo's cartoon disappeared not long after that.

His disgust at seeing two years' work dissolve through a last-minute error in judgment must have been easier for Leonardo to overcome at this time, because, apparently, he was emotionally involved with Mona Lisa, the young wife of a wealthy Florentine named Francesco del Giocondo. The novel by Dmitri Merejkowski has helped establish a romantic but unprovable legend about Leonardo and his relationship to the subject of the *La Gioconda* portrait. Beyond any doubt, though, Leonardo was magnificently obsessed with Mona Lisa. She was twenty-four when she began sitting for her portrait. She was past thirty when Leonardo completed it. He intended that the painting be a thing of loveliness and beauty. Musicians and readers of poetry were sometimes present at the sittings by his arrangement in hopes that the finished work would in some way be a product of the unified arts and thereby approach perfect beauty. Leonardo's patron became impatient with the time that was passing and demanded his wife's picture. But even after its completion Leonardo could not bring himself to part with it. He insisted that there was work still to be done to the canvas and took it with him when he left Florence.

Seven years before, Louis XII of France had entered Milan and immediately had marveled at the *Last Supper*, at the impressive clay statue of Sforza and at the intricate decoration of several ceilings and walls in the Milanese ducal palace. From that time, Leonardo had been an absentee favorite of the French monarch. In 1507 the French governor of Milan, Charles d'Amboise, requested that the Signoria of Florence permit Leonardo to return to Milan. But in the way stood the unfulfilled Council Chamber commission and the ruined mural. The French king himself intervened. "We have," he wrote the Signoria, "particular need of Maestro Leonardo da Vinci, painter, of your city of Florence."

Leonardo was more than willing to go. He had no heart to begin again on the Anghiari mural, and in all probability his infatuation for Mona Lisa, whether the woman or the painted image, was causing him anguish. He posted a bond against his failure to return (the bond would be forfeited) and was permitted to leave Florence.

In Milan, Leonardo at once turned his attention to engineering improvements in the Lombard canal system. Soon a member of an old Milanese family, Marshal Gian Giacomo Tribulzio, dispossessed by Lodovico and given back his citizenship rights by the conquering French, commissioned Leonardo to do another equestrian statue—of himself, the Marshal. Tribulzio had ardently admired the clay model of the Sforza monument. This time, he assured the sculptor, the statue would be cast. Leonardo accepted. This would be his answer to Michelangelo's barbed comment. But work never got beyond the planning stage. French rule soon ended in Milan and Marshal Tribulzio became too involved in the subsequent political changes to harry Leonardo for long about his monument.

Leonardo revisited Florence briefly to contest the disposition of the estate of his father who had died leaving no will. Then, not long after Leonardo's return to Milan, Louis XII of France re-entered the city. For a short time Leonardo was again a military engineer, campaigning with the French against Venice, the city he had once helped defend against the Turks. In between these military disturbances during the next four years Leonardo became tutor to a growing school of worshipful pupils. When he could, or would, he worked on *Leda and the Swan*. But by September, 1513, the French had been driven back across the Alps and Leonardo was again without a patron.

It was still the high noon of the Renaissance. Julius II, the militant Pope who added to the wealth and territory of the

37

Papacy, had just died. Giovanni de' Medici of Florence was elected to succeed him as Pope Leo X. This was a matter of great rejoicing for all the art world of the day. The Medici family, after all, had led Italy in its sympathetic support and patronage of art and learning. Where Julius had bullied Michelangelo into fantastic labors, as in the Sistine Chapel, he had as frequently frustrated and antagonized the artist in his work by such threats as swearing to throw him from the scaffolding if the commission was not finished by a date desired by the Pope. Leo, with the wealth and influence of his position as Pope would, it was felt, turn Italy into a great art studio. Rome, which was already benefiting gloriously from the blessings of the Renaissance, employing as it

St. Peter's Cathedral

was the brush and chisel of Michelangelo, promised to overtake and pass Florence as the cultural headquarters of the day under Leo X. The Pope's brother, Giuliano de' Medici, was brought to Rome to serve as governor of Papal territories as quickly as they could be won from their legitimate rulers. Giuliano then invited his family's old art protégé, Leonardo da Vinci, to come to Rome as an artist of the Papal court.

But Rome never belonged to Leonardo, or Leonardo to Rome. Giuliano, his benefactor, was sickly and gone from the city most of the time, engaged in useless wars for his brother, the Pope. The principal dispenser of art patronage was Leo X, and Leo's favorite was now Raphael who worked at the high speed desired by an impatient patron. Raphael, who had seemed destined to paint every room in the Vatican under Julius, was now assured of continuing his work under Leo. Michelangelo had been sent back to Florence by Leo to exercise his skill with marble on the facade of a church built by the Medici.

It could not have been Raphael's domination of the Roman art world that served to suppress Leonardo, the painter, there. Raphael did not forget the emotional, educational impact he had experienced at first seeing Leonardo's genius displayed on the pasteboard cartoon in Florence a decade earlier. It is said that in Raphael's Vatican fresco, the *School of Athens,* the serene Plato who points upwards to indicate the Ideal is a portrait of Leonardo. Raphael even turned some work in the direction of the master, but it was inconsequential: a small portrait or miniature for a wealthy citizen, perhaps.

No, the will to paint, too infrequently evident throughout his lifetime, was nearly extinct now in "the man of the universe." The *Mona Lisa* would be his last completed painting. His three years in Rome, passed in a secluded apartment, were spent in busy experiments with alchemy, plant life, and those of his art theories concerned with light and shade in painting. These notes were published posthumously as Leonardo's *Treatise on Painting*.

The French still asked for Leonardo, and when his benefactor, Giuliano, died in 1516, the man from Vinci journeyed across the Alps at the request of the new king of France, Francis I. At Cloux, near Amboise in Touraine, Leonardo was settled comfortably and honorably, now a royal protégé. He was sixty-four and the court painter by title, but he was making little or no attempt to finish his *Saint John the Baptist,* his final painting which would have to be completed by others later. In practice he was the court philosopher, and as able a pageant-master as he had been under Lodovico. He made another papier-mâché lion that exploded into a bouquet of lillies for the king and his entourage. Benvenuto Cellini was to write that Francis I "did not believe that any other man had ever been born into the world who knew so much as Leonardo, not only in sculpture, painting and architecture, but still more in that he was a very great philosopher."

Leonardo's right hand was crippled now, but he had been a left-handed artist and his investigations into science and nature must have gone on, although his notebooks came to an indifferent close in June, 1518. He died on May 2, 1519. The marking of his grave has long been lost, although a tomb to his memory—as though one were needed—was erected in the chapel of St. Blaise in France.

His death, far from the Tuscan hills of his birthplace, would not have mattered to Leonardo. His life and his works belonged from the beginning to all peoples who have sought understanding

Monument to Marcus Aurelius

and beauty. His allegiance was never to one city, nation or period of history. By the lamp of retrospect, western civilization has observed with wonder and dazed admiration as the lagging years have been seen to gradually catch up with Leonardo who labored so far in advance of his time. The mysteries that surround his story have only everything in common with the mysteries of universal genius that are always with us in one disguise or another. Vasari, eight years old at the time of Leonardo's death, groped to define the man and his deeds and decided that they nowhere touched upon grounds of mortal understanding. "Occasionally," Vasari wrote of Leonardo, "heaven sends us someone who is not only human but divine, so that through his mind and the excellence of his intellect we may reach out to heaven."

The words are ridiculous to anyone who has looked upon the mind and soul of Leonardo in his writings and his paintings that are left to us and has found nothing there. For others, the words seem at least to hint at that truth one is permitted to glimpse frequently—and even touch—but never quite comprehend.

Sketch of the Valley looking from Mt. Albino

C H A P T E R   I I I

Vinci

THE TUSCAN village of Vinci, where Leonardo was born, has only recently begun to awaken to its historical distinction. When Lumen Martin Winter visited the village in the spring of 1951 in search of the spirit of Leonardo the population was approximately a thousand people. The majority of its citizens were Communist sympathizers but its mayor was not. Vinci was not then within the regular tourist circuit of Italy. The speech-making and celebration of Leonardo's five hundredth birth anniversary would come the following year, setting the community aglow with a fresh and proud sense of importance. But in the spring of Winter's visit he found the unhurried pace of the village ideal for observing, sketching and meditating. He thought he saw the Mona Lisa in several of the high-cheekboned peasant women who walked the streets of Vinci. The glowing sunrises and sunsets still blanketed the hills in the blues and purples Leonardo painted so often in his portraits. Winter recognized the very landscape around Vinci as that which appeared in the background behind Christ and His disciples in the greatest of Leonardo's paintings.

There was one inn in town: the *Trattaria Leonardo*. It was there that Winter, lacking even a tourist's acquaintance with the Italian language, requested lodging and food by drawing pictures on his notepad for the innkeeper and his wife. And what quicker way to the heart of an Italian than through the art medium! This American, they told each other, was a *pictura,* a colorful character. A local resident sat near by while Winter ate his dinner. He would be most pleased, he told Winter, to interpret for him. English, he knew—a little at least. Enough. Was the American a tourist? Eh? A painter! And come to see for himself where the master Leonardo had lived! This information must be shared with the innkeeper and his wife.

Casa Leonardo

44

Town of Vinci

The story was straightaway shared. The keeper then held a whispered consultation with his wife and approached Winter. He was, he said, delighted to know the reason for the American's visit to their town. Perhaps the American would consent to a little practice at his profession before undertaking his most admirable of projects? The walls of his tavern were pitifully barren of artistic decoration, as the American could see. Hardly appropriate in the single hotel of Leonardo's birthplace, was it not true? If, by chance, the *signor* would care to paint a large fish and a bottle of wine on the wall . . . ?

Instead Winter drew a life-sized sketch of Leonardo's self-portrait—the wise face crowned with the abundant hair and adorned with the flowing beard. His model was a print he had

45

purchased in Florence. He had no sooner begun the chalk work than there was suddenly an audience of a hundred townspeople watching him. He finished the fresco, rubbing sienna into the plaster with his thumb. It had required three hours. A real labor of love could not be ended that quickly. So on the opposite wall he painted a copy of Leonardo's *La Gioconda*. Then he wrote the dedication in English: "In memory of Vinci, 1951, Lumen Winter."

This American, announced the innkeeper, would be a guest of the house during his stay in Vinci. These magnificent portraits, they were so much better than the fish or the wine.

These people of good will, appreciative and interested, appealed warmly to Winter. They, like the landscape, would be no strangers to Leonardo. In the village church was the baptismal font said to be the very one in which Leonardo was christened. Hugging one side of the rugged stone Vinci castle was the Leonardo museum, established under Mussolini. There Winter looked upon many of the da Vinci notebook manuscripts whose English translations had long been his treasured possessions. He studied the curious inverted left-handed script of Leonardo, script that must be held to a mirror to be read. Most of the books written *about* the universal man were gathered there, too, not all of which had been translated into English. The volunteer librarian was most happy to make the American's acquaintance and to learn the nature of his visit to Vinci. Was it not sad, *signor,* that the village does not own a single one of Leonardo's sketches, now the jewels of better known museums? But then, its stock of reproductions was growing. In fact, an American, Dr. Elmer Belt of Los Angeles, who was so enlightened as to start his own Leonardo museum as a hobby, has been generous enough to supply the Vinci library with all duplicates of items he has acquired. And he has sent nearly a hundred items. Is that not magnificent? One must not overlook Vinci, *signor,* in dealing with Leonardo. The American artist was well advised to come here. Leonardo returned in his mature days to visit his old home. One is ever a product of one's past, *signor,* is one not? The fact cannot be overlooked. The curator then demonstrated some of the models of Leonardo inventions—the armored car, the airplane—and for a moment Leonardo the artist was obscured by Leonardo the engineer.

It would not be overlooked. Up the road from Vinci, near Anchiano on the side of Monte Albino, was the Casa Leonardo, the house where, according to historical acceptance, the master spent most of his childhood. Winter's sense of sober dedication was not diminished by the fact that he made the pilgrimage to the Casa Leonardo on the rear of a motorcycle, driven by a hospitable vineyard owner.

It is a sound premise that a creative mind draws for its raw materials on the stores it acquired during childhood. To stand before the door of Leonardo's boyhood home, to turn slowly and see the Arno Valley that graces the backgrounds of his great paintings, is to be reminded of that premise. There is the winding road which wriggles its way through the backdrop of the *Last Supper* and the *Mona Lisa.* There is Mont Blanc and the whole Tuscan mountain range that were models for Leonardo's painted hills. The olive trees and the stony crags that filled the boy, Leonardo, with a metaphysical wonder at nature, live on today although their portraits fade in museums throughout Europe. At one's feet are the floral specimens and plants traced in the note-books. Winter plucked one fernlike herb. He vaguely associated it with something about Leonardo. He would recognize it at last when he began his replica of the *Last Supper*. The design of the plant, he would learn, strongly resembled that which embroiders the table cloth and wall tapestry of that upstairs room, where Christ and the disciples ate.

The house, when Winter sketched it inside and out, was ram-shackle. (The event of Leonardo's Quincentennial has since brought some attention to correcting its condition.) The door hung creakingly open. Moving through the lonely, barren rooms of the L-shaped house, Winter came across a wasp; the nest of a

Interior of Casa Vinci, birthplace of Leonardo

Leonardo discovering an effect of light and shadow

field mouse. Nothing more. The small windows still admitted the soft Italian sunshine Leonardo mentioned so often in his *Treatise on Painting*. They were, Winter noted, remarkably similar to the windows in the *Last Supper* chamber. The sagging beamed ceiling could as easily be imagined as those in that famous dining room. Winter's pockets were soon bulging with impromptu sketches he made throughout the house and in its court.

On the second floor of the house, the museum curator had told him, was Leonardo's room, according to common belief. And if it was, it was here in this murky, dusty room that the boy performed his first artistic feat: filling a panel of cypress wood with the image of a fantastic monster. The story is that the twelve-year-old boy pulled the draperies of the room and worked alone in the candle light for three days, studying a toad, a lizard and a snake for

The lock

physical features that he incorporated into his fire-vomiting creation.

On the ground floor, near the open door, Winter found and claimed as a souvenir rich in symbolism a rusty, iron, heavy lock that had been worn thin by the elements through five hundred years. It was exciting to stand in the doorway of the Casa Leonardo and meditate on the part this very lock might have played in the life of the child, Leonardo. For the metal was centuries old. A key that fitted the lock would have had to describe a complete circle. The memory of that key-turn might have come bounding back from the past to inaugurate Leonardo's idea for the helicopter plan, perhaps, with its perfect circle. The key turned on an axis, as Leonardo's screw-propeller would turn nearly fifty years after he had left the house. The frame of the original lock would have formed a square, and a peek through the hole would have filled da Vinci's observant eyes with the natural vistas he was to reproduce for the rest of his life. Perhaps, as he stood in the ray of light coming through the keyhole, he first considered his shadow on the far wall and there and then began his important inquiry into the relationship of light to shadow. For the moment at least it was enough for Winter that he could hold a simple functional object like a rusty lock and believe that it linked a common thought in minds separated by centuries.

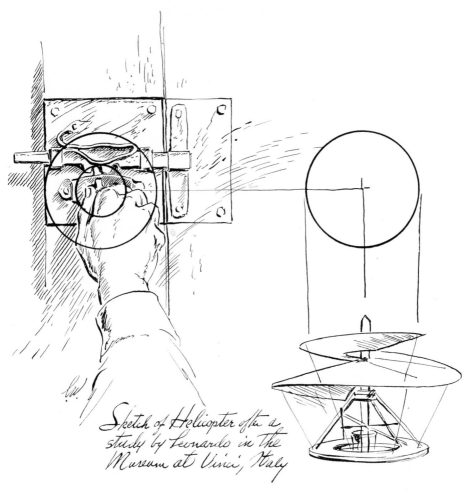

Sketch of a Helicopter after a study by Leonardo in the Museum at Vinci, Italy

Winter sat in the doorway and studied the ochre-colored soil, and the high-mountain grass flecked with red and white poppies. A peasant girl passed by, her hair the golden red that Leonardo's was supposed to be. The liquid brown eyes, that took him in in one curious glance, her face, her movements, were they, he wondered, of some traceable strain that produced Leonardo?

Rain began to fall on the return trip—this time on foot—to Vinci. Winter sought shelter under an olive tree and recognized the village and the few figures in the wet as a Leonardo sketch. He was not simply a fair-weather re-creator of the master's works.

Standing in the rain he drew the hamlet surrounding the Castle of Vinci and a few natives who passed by with their black umbrellas.

One last journey was made to the museum for another look at the fascinating inverted handwriting of Leonardo. Long before modern penetrating x-ray photographs of Leonardo's paintings confirmed the left-to-right diagonal course of the brush strokes, students of da Vinci had guessed his left-handedness from his handwriting. There was little else about Leonardo that was as easy to come by.

Rainy day in Vinci (*white spots in the picture were caused by the rain falling on Winter's sketch block*)

Sacre Coeur Cathedral in Paris

54

CHAPTER IV

The Art of Leonardo

WINTER spent six weeks in France and Italy examining the paintings of Leonardo that still live in one form of preservation or another. He knew the master's notebook sketches by heart—the baby pictured with surprising accuracy in the womb; a horse; a bird. There was no time or need to spend long in studying the originals of most of these drawings (collected at the Royal Library at Windsor Castle, England, and in the Abrosiana Library in Milan). The re-creation of the *Last Supper,* after all, had been promised Winter's patron within eight months. The form and composition of a penciled drawing was as readily evident in a good reproduction as in the original, but a painting was another matter. The authentic masterpieces had to be expertly scrutinized for technique, color, and surface characteristics. Careful color notes and sketches had to be made from these originals while museum guards and passersby stared curiously. And even then there were unanswered questions. So few of Leonardo's works had been completed by him. Where had he left off, and a pupil

55

finished? Prints of x-ray photographs of several Leonardo paintings were of immeasurable assistance to Winter in some cases, but in others the river of time had washed away certain secrets.

Of a few paintings there could be little doubt and these served Winter's cause well. One of the Louvre's prizes was the *Madonna of the Rocks*. The picture was later cleaned for the London exhibit of 1952, celebrating Leonardo's five hundredth anniversary, but when Winter spent hours inspecting it the previous year the colors had been greatly dimmed by the years' deposits. This, in fact, may have only extended the effect Leonardo intended. For Leonardo's original inspiration had been drawn from his early days in Vinci, and, later, in Milan when he would wander away by himself to explore the rocky caverns of the Italian hills. Nature, in its dark and lonely aspects, had filled him with fear and awe and had presented a pressing but insoluble mystery, he confessed one day in his notebooks. Dominant landscapes in religious paintings were still infrequent. And then, it was the Renaissance, and nature was supposed to be shown as wedded to man. So against the somber and rugged background of rocks and caverns, the Holy Virgin had taken shape. Those who wished to emphasize the doctrine of the Immaculate Conception had asked that the Virgin and Child be surrounded by angels and prophets, a typical theme of the period's religious art. But Leonardo deviated, wishing to preserve the sense of natural solitude. For a startling contrast against the rocks he painted the young Holy Mother and playful babies in a cheerful springtime mood.

Antonina Vallentin offers a moving description of this group in her biography, *Leonardo da Vinci:*

The Madonna of the Rocks (*with diagram of geometrical composition*)

The Blessed Virgin, moved by the gentleness of the spring day, has fallen on her knees, and is stretching her arms protectively round the playing children, who are untouched as yet by any shadow of the suffering world. Gravely, and inwardly radiant, she turns her face to the child John. He has bent his little round knee in the midst of flowers and grasses in their springtime glory, and is lifting up his fat little clasped hands to the divine Child, who is unsteadily raising his soft, helpless little body; the little pink foot on which the light burden weighs is bent round in a touchingly awkward position as he opens his tiny fist in benediction.

An angel robed in scarlet satin is at the side of the Infant Christ.

Leonardo began the *Madonna of the Rocks* at least ten years before the *Last Supper*, but work on the *Madonna* was dragged out until the picture couldn't have been long gone from Leonardo's mind when he began the famous Supper painting. Mary's outstretched hand has the same foreshortened quality to it that Leonardo gave Christ's hand at the Supper table.

The techniques used in painting the *Madonna* belong, in their simplest applications, to the most academic of art theories: the interplay of light and shade, called chiaroscuro, and perspective, the representation of objects or vistas on a flat surface as they would appear normally to the eye.

Leonardo wrote down for his own reference:

A painter should never tie himself to imitate the manner of any other; his business being not to represent the works of other men, but those of nature; who at the same time is so abundant in her productions, that it is ridiculous to have recourse to her servants, who have nothing but what they borrowed from her, when the mistress herself is so ready to entertain them.

Because he had been a student under Verrocchio, he had been taught the satisfaction to be found in a formally drawn line, and a composition of classical tradition. Leonardo's most obvious pioneering was in the stage-settings of his pictures. Pictorial backgrounds in paintings had been largely decorative. Former artists had played down light and shade, following the old rules that said a subject should not be made to look in a picture as it does to the human eye. They had placed their emphasis upon color and outline.

And so the three-dimensional illusion of the *Madonna of the Rocks* aided the revolution in art. The principals of the painting sit in a golden twilight. The highlights of the background, a flash of sky or water, stand forth. The observer, looking past the human figures, finds a continuity to the drama as he moves deeper and deeper into the composition.

Leonardo possessed so wondrous an admiration of the natural world he could only paint it as it appeared to human vision. The observer, he felt, must be able to recognize a painting as a faithful recording of things as they were. Sight, the only one of the senses painting appeals to, must be pampered in every way. "Painting is concerned with all the ten attributes of sight, namely darkness, brightness, substance and color, form and place, remoteness and nearness, movement and rest," da Vinci wrote. His more spec- tacular departures from artistic custom were in "darkness" and "brightness" (chiaroscuro) and "remoteness and nearness" (per- spective).

Leonardo's ideas for his paintings were usually suggested by his sponsors. The pictures' conceptions were intuitive with Leo- nardo. But the basis of their construction was mathematics. "Study mathematics," Leonardo once commanded his students, "and do not build without foundations." The central pattern of the *Madonna of the Rocks* is an unmistakable equilateral triangle, its apex at the top of Mary's head. One side of the triangle leads from Mary's hair through her hand, which rests on the infant John's shoulder, and then down to the child's foot. The other side of the geometrical figure runs to the angel's robe.

The large collection of sketches that Lumen Winter accumulated, standing in the Louvre before the *Madonna of the Rocks, Saint Anne with the Virgin and Child, Saint John the Baptist* and the *Mona Lisa,* would have made little or no sense to one trying to associate the strange geometrical figures and color splotches on his note pads with the masterpieces he was studying. And then there were the hours spent in just looking at the paintings without making notes. For no notes could catch and hold those mystical qualities Leonardo worked into his pictures through glazing, brushing and surface construction. These things were tied up with da Vinci's nervous system and his senses; his heart and not his mind. Winter could but memorize their effects upon him; to articulate for himself his own emotional reactions to this great art as best he could and hope that he could summon it to the surface of his consciousness when he should perhaps need it to explain a face, a hand, a foot in the *Last Supper*.

Leonardo began his *Saint Anne and the Virgin* about 1500. He had just returned to Florence from Milan after Lodovico's overthrow. He was then forty-eight and had begun the work as an altar piece intended for the Church of the Annunciation. The Order of the Servites, his commissioners, had given him a quiet monastery cell in which to work. But before he had fairly begun

60

Saint Anne with the Virgin and Child *with geometrical analysis*

he became absorbed in the mathematical theories of his friend, Fra Luca Pacioli, who persuaded Leonardo to draw the diagrams for his book, *Of Divine Proportion*. The impatient monks finally hurried Leonardo into beginning *St. Anne and the Virgin* but the work shows his decided obsession with geometry. The pyramid of people is so concentrated that Mary sits on the lap of Saint Anne who, in turn, watches while the Virgin gently restrains the Blessed Child, occupied with a lamb. Leonardo's beloved landscape stretches into the background with all the props of nature he took with him from Vinci: mountain peaks, the valley, and a conifer tree silhouetted against twilight shades.

In some ecclesiastical circles the painting has been taken to be allegorical. Saint Anne is interpreted as representing the mother church. Mary attempts to rescue her Child (unsuccessfully) from His central interest, the lamb (His earthly mission) which will lead him eventually to fulfill all the prophecies of pain and miracles to come.

Leonardo's valleys, streams and broken hilly country appear again in the backdrop of the *Mona Lisa*. They comprise the only real adornment of the painting. The ungarnished hair of the woman falls down to an ungarnished gown. And even the landscape detracts little from the lovely facial expression. Her colors have faded in spite of the attempts to rescue them, but the expression prevails. The personal emotions that Leonardo so zealously kept out of his notebooks he seemed to pour willingly into this portrait. "The lover is drawn by the thing loved," he recorded once, "as the sense is by that which it perceives, and it unites with it, and they become one and the same thing. The work is the first thing born of the union . . ." Talk as he might of an

Even in his most sentimental painting, the Mona Lisa, *Leonardo applied the theory of mathematics*

artist's fidelity to nature, his loyalties during the painting of the *Mona Lisa* must have been drawn to natural forces with no immediate bearing on his theories of art. The *Mona Lisa* remains Leonardo's one supreme example of romanticized reality.

Leonardo's last picture, *Saint John the Baptist*, was probably executed in Florence between 1509 and 1512. The original has long since been lost and the Louvre painting is thought to have been copied from the Leonardo original, or a sketch, by one of his pupils: Desare da Sesto. The title of the piece was changed to *Bacchus* in a later, prudish age, that became scandalized over John, who was posed as a young nude in the wilderness, bearing a cross and beckoning to the world he hoped to baptize. The sensuousness was there, beyond any doubt, and it needed only a leopard skin around the hips to transform John into the pagan god of wine with a vine-wreath on his head. The cross was changed into a symbolic staff—a thyrsus. Like the other Leonardo panels in the Louvre, it was painted in egg and oil emulsion on gesso ground, well preserved with varnish. And on none of the canvases were there brush strokes showing.

Florence still shimmers with the dust of the golden age of the Renaissance when she was host to Michelangelo, Cellini and Machiavelli. But she is custodian now of only three da Vinci creations—all performed in the dawn of his career. The gallery of the Uffizi Palace houses the *Baptism of Christ,* Verrocchio's commission which the pupil Leonardo helped to complete. An angel in the lower left corner of the altar piece was probably done by Leonardo. The figure bears the same heavy, serious-minded qualities of Verrocchio's style, which the apprentice, Leonardo, would seek to imitate. But the surrounding light-and-shade relationships suggest that Leonardo was already exploring in a new direction. The rare sensitive touch to the face of Christ is thought to be another clue to the extent of Leonardo's participation. Christ's head is centered in the panel and turned at nearly the same angle as in the *Last Supper*. This may have been Verrocchio's arrangement in the *Baptism,* or it may have meant the teacher was already listening to his precocious assistant.

In his early days in Florence Leonardo painted a *predella,* or a strip-picture, as the bottom border of an altar piece. It tells the story of the Angel Gabriel reverently bringing the message of the Incarnation to Mary. Both figures are in a kneeling position, their eyes cast down. Leonardo's recognizable landscape is seen from a lower angle which emphasizes the silhouettes of the Italian pine trees and the peaked hills and which all but misses the usual meandering stream. The most spectacular fact about the *Angel of the Annunciation* is that Leonardo engineered the wings of Gabriel not as legendary symbols but as authentic bird's wings capable, beyond any doubt, of lifting the weight of the angel's body to which they are attached.

To the confusion of art experts for a time, a second *Angel of the Annunciation,* once thought to be by Leonardo, is in existence, now at the Louvre. The majority opinion today holds that this second strip-painting was modeled after one of Leonardo's preliminary sketches of his *Annunciation,* possibly by a student whom Leonardo may have assisted, or by Verrocchio, who was still in close association with Leonardo at the time the work was performed. The preliminary drawing, possibly used as a model, is at Christ Church College in Oxford, England.

The third of Leonardo's pieces at the Uffizi museum promised to be one of his greatest masterpieces, had he completed it before leaving Florence for Milan at the age of thirty. Bernard Berenson, however, author of *The Drawings of the Florentine Painters,* describes this work—the *Adoration of the Magi*—as "happily unfinished."

The subject of the kings arrived to worship the newborn Christ Child was a popular one with earlier Italian masters, and Botticelli had just completed one for the Santa Maria Novella in Florence. Leonardo hewed to the Renaissance custom of picturing Mary holding the Child, not in a manger, but in a regal hall of classical architecture. A host of people strain to see the Infant, or stand in wonder and adoration. Noble white horses of foreign princes prance in the background, as if instinctively aware of the miracle. For Leonardo charged this painting with all the promise of vital dramatic movement and mystical atmosphere he would fulfill in later pictures. His use of chiaroscuro, light and shade was already highly skilled.

Considering Lumen Winter's immediate aims, the *Adoration of the Magi* proved ideal. For practically every stage of Leonardo's work on the canvas is revealed in some area of it. There are the first outlines of the Holy Child on the gesso ground surface; higher up are the horses of a more complete composition. The whole painting is done in brown and amber monochrome. And yet the work is aesthetically complete in itself. So frequently in art it is the first draft, the rapid sketch, that expresses the idea clearly and compactly. An artist does not give himself enough time in that

Adoration of the Magi

early stage of a painting to overstate his theme or exaggerate his points, or to detract from essences with gaudy colors. Rembrandt, who especially admired the *Adoration,* might conceivably have been less impressed had the painting's middle-tones—the umber under-painting—been covered by an orthodox finish.

It may be poetically just that Rome, so ungenerous with Leonardo, boasts only one painting by the master, and that, un-completed. *St. Jerome* which, in its badly damaged state, hangs in the Vatican was executed by Leonardo in Florence during the same period that produced the *Adoration*. In approximately the same state of incompleteness as the *Adoration, St. Jerome* seems to represent Leonardo's own despair about the time he painted the piece. Leonardo was suffering then from slanderous moral charges by several Florentines. It could well explain why Saint Jerome is depicted as a revolting old man who kneels at the entrance to a dark grotto. He holds a stone aloft, about to strike it against his chest. His bald head resembles that of a mummy and his pose and attitude strongly suggests an impulse of self-destruction. This stark image of the saint may have been the projection of the young embittered Leonardo—a self-portrait twisted to personify frustration or an expiation of guilt. Or was Leonardo, the detached observer, always the master of his subjective self? Was it merely an experiment at showing how a distraught man may look? "A man who is in despair," Leonardo had written in his notebook, "you should make turning his knife against himself, and rending his garments with his hands, and one of his hands should be in the act of tearing open his wound."

There were other things in Rome for Winter to note. Leonardo, he realized, must have found the architecture engaging. The Roman buildings then, as now, abounded in spheres, cubes, and triangles, circles, pyramids and cones, adhering to the Greek rule of imitating forms found in nature. There were the works of Raphael to be examined and influences of Leonardo's mysterious art mannerisms upon Raphael to be sifted out. And Pope Pius, who had somehow heard of Winter's distinguished mission, invited the American to a special audience during which he blessed the undertaking. How appropriate that the successor to the papal

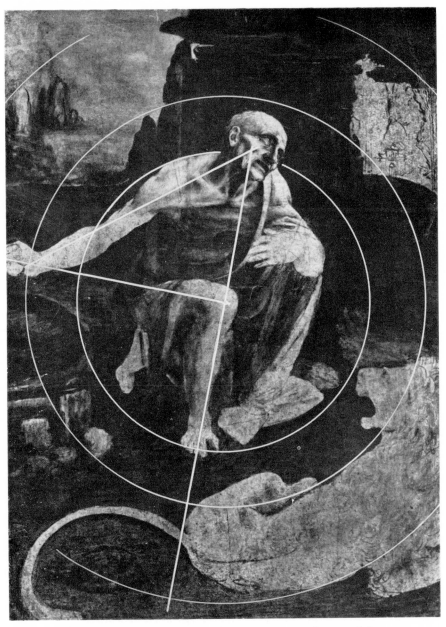

St. Jerome (*definitely constructed on the circle*)

heads who had once controlled and directed so much of Renaissance art should in some way participate in an attempt to re-create one of its greatest examples.

MILAN '51

The Church of Santa Maria delle Grazie

The Church of Santa Maria delle Grazie

AMONG MANY well-known artists who chose to paint the Lord's Last Supper were, besides Leonardo, Ghirlandaio, Andrea del Castagno, Andrea del Sarto, Tintoretto, Hans Holbein the younger, Nicholas Poussin, Duccio di Buoninsegna and Francesco Botticini. At the time Lumen Winter looked upon the greatest version in the Santa Maria delle Grazie in Milan, da Vinci's *Last Supper* had been copied by twelve artists, either during Leonardo's lifetime or within a few years after his death when the mural was still all but perfectly preserved. The best known copy was done by Marco d'Oggiono, one of Leonardo's devoted pupils. Copied originally for the Certosa at Pavia, it is now in the London collection of the Royal Academy. All copies, including d'Oggiono's, were somewhat modified, and several of them were insignificant. None were full-sized duplicates.

Leonardo chose to paint the story of the Supper at its climax, the moment of Christ's prediction of the betrayal by Judas. Jesus had sent Peter and John ahead to make arrangements for Him and the disciples to feast on the passover. The goodman of a house led them to a large, furnished upper room where the two apostles set the table. "I have desired to eat this passover with you before I suffer," Christ told His disciples. And when the meal had been eaten, Christ startled the group by announcing: "One of you shall betray me."

The Bible (John: 13:22) describes the pregnant occasion Leonardo was to immortalize pictorially:

> Then the disciples looked on one another, doubting of whom he spake.
> Now there was one leaning on Jesus' bosom one of his disciples, whom Jesus loved. [John]
> Simon Peter therefore beckoned to him, that he should ask who it should be of whom he spake.
> He then lying on Jesus' breast saith unto him, Lord, who is it?
> Jesus answered, He it is, to whom I shall give a sop, when I have dipped *it*. And when he had dipped the sop, he gave *it* to Judas Iscariot, the son of Simon.
> And after the sop, Satan entered into him. Then said Jesus unto him, That thou does, do quickly.
> Now no man at the table knew for what intent he spake this unto him.
> For some of them thought, because Judas had the bag, that Jesus had said unto him, buy those things that we have need of against the feast; or, that he should give something to the poor. He then having received the sop went immediately out: and it was night.

The fact that it was night only a few moments after Christ's announcement was interpreted by Leonardo, apparently, to have been a sudden ending of day at the Lord's bidding. The artist from Vinci would not be denied his Italian landscape of a winding river and broken terrain which, lit by the light of day, reaches into the distance through the windows of the upper room, behind the holy men.

Leonardo exercised his artist's license in another way: the entire group of men is assembled in his painting along the far side and the two ends of the table, a most impractical eating arrangement since all thirteen could not possibly have enough room in which to seat themselves. And yet, how could he be expected to paint only the backs of any one of such exalted men?

At the left of Leonardo's dramatic panorama is Nathaniel Bartholomew who starts to his feet in astonishment, but with disbelief mixed with his surprise. At his left is the younger James. James reaches in back of Andrew, who sits to his left, and touches Peter, perhaps to ask if he has heard aright. Andrew has thrown up his hands, aghast, and looks toward Christ for some elaboration or explanation of His remark. Judas Iscariot, treasurer of the group, leans morosely away from Christ, clutching the bag of money that a moment later would mislead the others as to the reason for his departure from the room. Peter, the big fisherman, bluff and excitable as always, angrily grasps a knife and has pulled John toward him to ask who the betrayer might be. John, whom Christ loved most, is appropriately seated beside the Master. His unperturbed sorrow indicates that he might have suspected Christ's forthcoming accusation. Jesus Christ is the radiant central figure, silhouetted within the frame of the center window. His detachment from the rest of the faces, shoulders and arms would attract an observer's attention immediately. The bright red robe

He wears would be an over-emphasis by normal art standards. There is an obscure incommunicable expression on the face of Christ. His arms rest wearily on the table, the right hand in the classical pose of benediction, the other in the upturned gesture of fatal acceptance. The doubting Thomas has pushed toward Christ, his index finger upraised, seeking more details connected with the betrayal indictment. James, the Elder, beseechingly holds out his arms and asks, "Lord, is it I?" Shy, emotional Philip has arisen in his sudden anguish, has placed his hands to his breast and on the point of tears is protesting his innocence. "Thou knowest, Lord, that it is not I." Matthew and Simon, at the right of the table, are both talking and gesturing, Matthew pointing toward Christ, perhaps repeating the fatal words. Thaddeus, looking distressed, is concentrating on what Simon is saying.

It is less obvious today that the high-beamed ceiling of the chamber in the picture is an extension of the old monastic dining room, which would have made the refectory long indeed. For the extension would have led on through Christ's banquet chamber and out the open windows to the distant hazy horizons of Leonardo's landscape. And the long trestled table of the painting, draped with its newly unfolded cloth of blue embroidery, was undoubtedly modeled after the refectory table of the monks.

Now, only the ghost of Leonardo's *Last Supper* lingers in the church of Santa Maria delle Grazie. (André Malraux once assigned the work to "the privileged class of glorious ruins.") To an artist seeking to reproduce the work, what remains for him to see has been made untrustworthy by well-intentioned artists in the past who hoped to restore the painting or impede its rate of decay but who more frequently aided its deterioration by using harmful ingredients or applying second-rate art on the filling of vacant or faded patches in the mural.

Fortunately for Winter, Leonardo's preparations had begun long before he went to Milan from Florence, or could have foreseen such a commission. He apparently had planned a *Last Supper* during most of his early career, and several of his preparatory sketches for the painting are still preserved. An early drawing (now in the Louvre) dating from Leonardo's first Florentine period is of a group of men and boys conversing around a long, narrow table. Christ, in another sketch on the same paper, is illustrated with His index finger pointing in a gesture of accusation.

Leonardo would have drawn a numberless amount of preparatory sketches for the Supper mural before satisfying himself with the groupings, poses and balances of the construction as it finally emerged. One early pen-and-ink sketch of the scene shows Judas sitting by himself on the near side of the table, being handed a cup by Christ. Other Renaissance artists painted their Last Suppers in this manner. A lovely drapery study in black and white by Leonardo appears to be the sleeve of Peter. Bartholomew, Judas, Philip, James and the clasped hands of John are presented charmingly in either red or black chalk in the Windsor Castle Leonardo collection. They serve as significant references to what the *Last Supper* components were once like.

It is not known whether Leonardo requested a wall in the refectory of the monastery as a proper place on which to paint his Supper scene, but from his early studies it is known that he felt compelled in some way to paint it one day, somewhere. Perhaps he conceived the idea in that period that produced his *St. Jerome,* when persecution by fellow citizens led him to distrust all men.

75

He would have found comfort in realizing that Christ, Himself, had recognized the unreliability of human nature, had suffered because of it, and had finally triumphed over it. That moment of betrayal, then, he might have decided, must be painted for all the ages to come.

The public of Milan came and went in the refectory, visited and passed on, always maintaining a gallery of spectators from the day Leonardo began transferring his sketches for the Supper mural to the refectory wall. The scene was first outlined in red chalk.

The prior of the monastery, Bandello, had a nephew, Matteo, who would one day write romantic Italian novels. As a youth, Matteo witnessed the painstaking construction of the great painting. He later wrote:

> Leonardo often came to work at an early hour of the morning, and promptly clambered up onto the scaffolding, for the *Last Supper* is situated at a considerable height above the floor; his practice was to work brush in hand until late in the evening, taking no thought for food or drink, but painting without cease. Then two, three or four days would go by without his touching his brush, though he spent one or two hours daily gazing at what he had done; he was turning it over in his mind, ruminating and debating with himself. . . . Yet I have also seen him (when the mood took him) come in at mid-day, take up the brush, give a few dabs to one of the figures, turn and go off again.

Leonardo worked regularly with living models. For Renaissance religious art was a thoughtful, careful craft drawn from everyday reality. Speaking of this period in art history, Antonina Vallentin wrote: "The saints concealed behind the flicker of the altar candles were artisans or shopkeepers from the neighborhood; the Madonnas bending over their chubby-faced children displayed the mother's pride of young Florentine women . . ."

We know more of how Leonardo must have worked from Giovanni Battista Giraldi who recorded, not long after Leonardo's death:

> Leonardo, as soon as he prepared to paint any figure, considered first its quality and nature, whether it should be noble or plebeian, gay or severe, troubled or cheerful, good or malignant; and when he had grasped its nature he set out for places where he knew that people of that sort gathered together, and diligently observed their faces, their manners, their habits, their movements; and as soon as he had found anything that seemed suited to his purpose he noted it with his pencil in the little book which he carried at all times in his girdle. My father, who took great interest in these things, told me thousands of times that Leonardo employed this method in particular for his famous painting in Milan.

Christ and Judas were the last figures Leonardo painted. He walked the streets of Milan searching the passing faces for the special qualities he wanted and for a time was unable to find them. "Your Excellency is aware that Judas is missing," Leonardo is said to have told Lodovico when the duke inquired the reason for the unfinished faces. "I cannot find features fit for so abandoned a character," Leonardo explained, referring still to Judas. "I have been going every day, morning and evening, for more than a year to the criminal quarter, in which the scum of humanity live; but I have not yet found what I want." Then he added defensively: "Not a day passes but I devote at least two hours to the work."

He sought the face of Christ among the duke's clean-cut courtiers and among the young Milanese noblemen. He finally settled on a man named "Cardinal del Mortaro" to be the model for the divine face. Christ's hands were painted in the image of those belonging to a young man named Allessandro. The spiritual significance of Christ's expression that confounded Leonardo so long may have been achieved finally through inspiration the artist acquired from a famous martyrdom at that time. The monk, Savonarola, had antagonized the worldly minded majority of the clergy with his preachings against the low morals of the times. His power over the people, rather than his loud protests against the corrupt monks and cardinals, frightened the church hierarchy. The Pope was persuaded to order Savonarola's death. The monk was burned alive in the public square of Florence in 1498. Leonardo, in nearby Milan, would soon have heard the news and such news might well have provided him with the powerful meaning of holy martyrdom that still shines gloriously from the face of Christ in the faded *Last Supper*. Leonardo would have found such a contemporary emotional force as worthy of preserving in an historical painting as the figures of his fellow-citizens, dead these four hundred years and more.

At last, in 1498, the painting was finished. Its unveiling helped mark the beginning of an art era and the decline of the *quattrocento* school of artists. Leonardo's loving attention given to perspective and shadow and light rendered the fictitious arrangement of thirteen people crowded unnaturally behind a table not only believable but as though it might have been divinely authorized. For even now, there is an abundant spiritual significance in the tattered remains of the *Last Supper*. A man such as Leonardo could not spend a life-time inquiring into cosmic matters without artistically acknowledging the holiness of creation. "That man becomes happy who follows Christ," he had written early in his diary. Throughout his records runs a respectful awareness of God's evidence.

The most daring quality to his Supper mural was that of giving every figure and face in the picture a separate pose which clearly implied the psychological impact of Christ's announcement upon the mind of each. A man's physical reflexes were the direct results of an inner motivation, most artists of the day realized, but few believed it possible to convey to art observers through pose and expression private thoughts of painted subjects experiencing an emotional crisis. But Leonardo quietly set down his beliefs on the matter in his *Treatise on Painting:* "A good painter," he wrote, "has two chief objects to paint, man and the intention of his soul; the former is easy, the latter hard because he has to represent it by the attitudes and movements of the limbs."

For years it had been supposed that Leonardo worked the *Last Supper* in oil paints, but with the advent of x-ray cameras it was discovered that he had been up to his old tricks of experimenting. He had used an emulsion of three parts egg, one part oil, which he painted on a thin plaster gesso ground, whose properties, he had hoped, would make the mural more permanent. At that, the mixture might have stood up laid on a wood panel, but not over wet plaster. The concoction dried hard, harder than the usual whitewash ground usually used as a foundation coat. Then it contracted on the damp wall of the refectory, curled and began to flake off. This process of obliteration began within a decade, well before Leonardo's death. It must have given the artist cause to

79

wonder if any representative fragment of his life's work would survive.

During one of the later French invasions, the Milanese refectory was used as a stable for the foreign cavalry. The military mind, ever quick to sacrifice a heritage of art for an expediency of the moment, decided that a stable door should be cut through the mural wall. By good fortune, the painting's lower edge begins nine feet from the floor and the door pierces only part of the hanging table cloth and eliminates only the feet of Christ and those of several of the centrally located disciples.

As the world turned and the decades passed, fine grains and scales of paint and plaster fell from the face of the wall. Smoke from an adjacent kitchen may have helped darken the masterpiece and flood waters are thought to have once inundated the room of the *Last Supper*. Its decay gradually increased, becoming more and more noticeable even to the unpracticed eye.

In 1726 an Italian artist named Bellotti tried to restore the work. Mistakenly believing it had been painted in oil, Bellotti covered Leonardo's mural with clear oil hoping to bring the dull colors to life. The result was a misfortune. In 1770, Mazza tried his luck with no better success and in 1819 Barezzi joined the ranks of those unequal to the task of restoring genius. Meanwhile, the harmful varnishes and glues were leaving their marks.

Finally, in 1853, Cavaliere Cavenaghi meticulously gathered up all he could find of the fallen particles from the disintegrating painting, using a pair of tweezers. He next cleaned the surface of as much foreign matter as could be safely removed and then glued into the bare patches all the bits of painting he had, fixing them with tempera. While cleaning the wall he uncovered a decorative border of lovely painted lunettes and vaultings above the upper edge of the mural. This dividend by Leonardo had been quite forgotten. The blue vaultings bore superimposed stars, and the lunettes were intertwined with knot ornaments and scutcheons.

When a bomb struck the church of Santa Maria delle Grazie during the second world war, blowing out the two side walls of the refectory, the Milanese took it for granted that Leonardo's roving spirit of the universe had intervened to save the wall painted with the *Last Supper* as well as the rear wall bearing Montorfano's fresco (the *Crucifixion*), finished just before Leonardo's mural.

The *Last Supper*'s survival, even in its present scarred condition, is felt by its present custodians to be a miracle worthy of the most scrupulous guardianship. To the museum's curator and the head of the Milanese Bureau of Education in 1951, the American artist who requested the chance to examine the sacred painting close up was highly suspect. Did Mr. Winter believe for a moment they would assist him in exploiting this work of genius for commercial interest? Ah, the American does not stand to profit from his replica of the *Last Supper*! The *signor* refers to his intentions as—how does he say—a labor of love? A pilgrimage in self-education? Pretty words, to be sure, but—eh? Eh? A chance for the *Last Supper* to be born again, and in America, you say. A gift? Ah, we see. A gift, so to speak, from Italy to the United States. A heritage of art, one might say, to unite the old world with the new, eh, *signor? Bene! Bene!*

With good wishes for his success, Winter was granted the services of two museum guards who helped him erect scaffolding before the mighty face of the famous painting. The scaffolding was borrowed from the workmen busy with repairing the damaged walls of the church. For three days Winter worked, measuring the dimensions of the mural, and the blurred objects and figures within the picture, ever careful not to touch the wall. To the tourists who filed through the museum, kept at a discreet distance by the guards, the small figure of Winter on the scaffolding must have emphasized the size and grandeur of the fresco.

Prints of x-ray photographs which Winter was able to purchase in Milan revealed the use of emulsion on the *Last Supper*. (The modern device of x-ray had similarly corrected the fallacy that El Greco painted in oil.) Winter used a lithograph of the original *Last Supper* (made in Milan about 1940) in order to work out the geometrical designs upon which Leonardo had based his construction.

The colors were more baffling. The tones in the Leonardo paintings at the Louvre had been immeasurably better preserved than in the Supper fresco. But the *Last Supper*'s six restorations confused Winter for a time as to what the colors had been like originally.

On the opposite wall, however, shone Montorfano's *Crucifixion* in secco fresco. This, the rear wall, had been done first by Montorfano. And Leonardo, Winter reasoned, being above all a picture painter and an art decorator would surely have chosen his colors for the *Last Supper* to blend with, or even match, those of his colleague's in the same room. And so Winter added careful color notes of the *Crucifixion* to his ever-increasing collection. To keep with him a touch of atmosphere from the old refectory's interior, Winter took the time to sketch the damaged room in free hand.

Little else could now be done for the original *Last Supper*,

Winter knew. A humidifier in the chamber tried to keep the damp air a little drier; sought to reduce the mural's further flaking. But nothing would save it. Winter placed himself at a distance from the painting for one last study before leaving Milan. When he had first looked upon the Supper scene he had stood for a half-hour transfixed and dumbfounded. It was no less thrilling now after three days of constant association with it. He tried to wipe clean the negative of his mind and give it a time exposure. He had to remember how the great mural looked in the fresh pale glow of

Sketch of the Refectory

morning, the brighter light of noon and in that mystical Italian twilight Leonardo loved best. He tried to imagine the clean, glimmering colors of the painting as they were when Leonardo first applied them. Perhaps the work had then needed a little of the venerability that age later gave it. The historical moment of the Supper had acquired a more mysterious importance with its darkened hues than its admirers of 1498 could ever have foreseen. The color-effects of the Supper's flaked and broken surface reminded Winter of a Seurat, or a Monet. It was still contemporary art after all the centuries. It was still of the universe.

The Parthenon, a perfect example of the sphere and cube

84

The Re-Creation

IN A FRENZY of endeavor, Lumen Winter completed his reproduction of Leonardo's *Last Supper* in December, 1951, less than eight months after the work had been commissioned. Caught up in the fascinating problems and rediscoveries that go with reproducing greatness, Winter found himself working fifteen hours a day, seven days a week. He did not dare relinquish the painting for long for fear some idea he held about the work would slip away; some psychological insight would be lost; some universal recognition might fade with hesitation. The New York studio on lower Fifth Avenue was suitable. There was still the large stretcher and backing Winter had used to paint the savings bank mural. That mural had measured fourteen by twenty-eight feet, only two inches shorter and seven inches more narrow than the *Last Supper*. The new clean canvas, sixteen by thirty feet, had to be rolled up as the sketching began, to permit the artist to get at the bottom of the picture.

He was able to incorporate from the beginning those basic factors that must have pre-occupied Leonardo for a great while: the grouping of the figures in the picture, the selection of poses assigned to each one, and the fundamental construction as a whole. For a fundamental thing about a painting is its construction, and the *Last Supper*'s construction was still discernible for all that portions of the background and bottom foreground were missing. Winter had read Leonardo's *Treatise on Painting* until he could recite sizable passages from it from memory. And in reading the book it seemed to Winter that to set himself back five centuries in the world of art was not much more than to turn back the hands of one's watch five minutes. Because perfection in art technique is changeless if time is not.

Winter employed three assistants, each specialists in still-lifes, or human figures or intricate brush work. Leonardo, like most artists of his day, had used helpers. The four better known are still honored by their statues at the base of Leonardo's monument in the public square of Milan. "It is much better to be in the company of others when you draw rather than alone," Leonardo wrote. To such a mind as his, even the errors of others might provide a new idea or a novel technique. Furthermore, he felt, art could live on properly only if one generation of artists passed on its methods to its successors.

Borrowing pictorial slides of Leonardo's *Last Supper* from the New York Metropolitan Art Museum, Winter was able to throw a few segments of the painting onto his canvas through a Balopticon projector. He then lightly traced these figures and objects in blue chalk. Keeping in mind the relationship of the segments as they appeared in the original picture, Winter next squared their dimensions algebraically and finally adjusted their proportions until they matched the exact measurements of Leonardo's subjects in the Milan refectory. With these forms to guide him, Winter used red chalk to draw the outlines of Christ and the disciples. He used freehand drawing (as did Leonardo) to avoid the static quality that too often comes from direct tracing. Making good use of the preliminary sketches Leonardo had made for the *Last Supper*, Winter rendered many drawings of his own in pencil before returning to his canvas chalking. His chalk work was done steadily and swiftly to get an even flow of lines and expression.

Ordinarily this would be risky business, but Winter had specialized in the study of human anatomy at several art schools. His collection of Leonardo's anatomical sketches had been acquired while attending the Academy in the shadow of the Cathedral of Saint John the Divine. And at the Cleveland School of Art, Winter had taken advantage of the chance to attend the medical school at Western Reserve University in order to witness and note actual dissections of human cadavers. That, too, was in the tradition of Leonardo who in his day had been far from faint-hearted in acquiring scientific knowledge with which to arrive at technical perfection in art. In a time that generally forbade such practices, Leonardo dissected as many as thirty human bodies in order to learn the sinews and joints responsible for particular postures and muscular actions.

Leonardo believed for a time that there were ten anatomical types among people, each type easily determined by only one physical feature: a chin or a forehead, for example. Winter had partly subscribed to this theory. (He has demonstrated that he need be shown only a man's nose in order to draw the rest of the face free-hand and make it recognizable.) He found nearly all Leonardo's ten types of faces in the *Last Supper*.

Winter was still in the anatomy-conscious phase of his career when he became a commercial artist in New York, his Leonardo notes and sketches on anatomy never far from his drawing board.

87

"You draw like a professor of anatomy," his first employer had once reproved him. And the man had been correct. Winter had been merely adding realistic surface dressings to his skeletons, or skinless figures. Long after falling into styles of his own, Winter paints a human figure today "from the inside to the outside."

One can only imagine the number of times Leonardo arranged and rearranged the figures and stage props in order to create the rhythmical balance of the *Last Supper*. He had the eye and hand of an artist, but the mind of a scientist. The design was probably inspired by the room where the mural was painted. Leonardo was well versed in the Greek principle of perfect symmetry, so admired by Renaissance artists, architects and sculptors. There is the same formal division in the background behind the holy men whose movements in the picture are never allowed to disturb the balance.

Winter was fully aware that Leonardo, at the time of his Supper's creation, was an eager student of geometry. Winter had read a translation of the book, *de Divina Proportione,* which Leonardo helped Fra Luca Pacioli, a mathematics professor in Milan, to produce. But Winter was scarcely prepared to discover the extent of geometrical theories Leonardo applied to his most famous masterpiece. For one thing, it developed that Leonardo had used a ground plan in order to obtain the effect of the mural's being an elongation of the actual dining room. Few artists bother with a ground plan, which is similar to an architect's blue-print. The refectory in Milan was seventy-nine feet long and Winter deduced by measurement and geometrical reduction that Leonardo's original viewpoint had been taken seventy-eight and a half feet away. The great man must have crowded his back against the opposite wall and allowed for a half-foot between the wall and the front of his head. Winter, who had made the discovery in Milan, took his stand in the same central position against the opposite wall and confirmed that the mural gives the most convincing illusion of being a room-extension at that distance.

Leonardo applied his "divine proportion" ratio to every relationship. Like the Greeks, he began with the premise that the lesser part of an unequally divided line is to the greater part as the greater part is to the entire line. This theory of graduation had already been devised by Leonardo of Pisa, an Italian mathematician living two centuries before Leonardo da Vinci. His theory, which da Vinci learned and employed, is called the "Fibonacci Series." Simply, it goes:

Designate a point in a design as "1".

Repeat this number and add it to the first number, making "2".

Add this number to the preceding one, making "3".

Add this number to the preceding one, making "5".

Add this number to the preceding one, making "8".

And so on.

In two-dimensional drawing, Leonardo used this ratio in determining the proper distances between objects, and to help maintain the formal balance of his paintings. Using a pair of dividers, Winter uncovered the fact that the wrinkles in Philip's robe were spaced apart in a ratio of two to three to five, as were the folds of Christ's robe.

For his own benefit Leonardo had accumulated a few rules of thumb regarding the human form in art. "The length of the ear," he wrote, "should equal the distance from the bottom of the nose to the top of the eyelid." And elsewhere in his notebooks: "The space between the eyes is equal to the size of one eye."

But knowing when and where to keep or break laws in creative-

Leonardo's theories of perspective were later applied by Matisse.

ness is frequently the difference between a genius and merely an art technician. For Leonardo didn't always follow his rules to their mathematical conclusions. Winter found one example of this fact in the case of the tapestries hanging on the two side walls of the banquet room, nearly obscured in the one good print of the original that was available. The design of the tapestries was strikingly like that of a species of plant Winter had noticed growing around the Leonardo house in Vinci. It also had a touch of the Orient in its pattern. (Italy was conducting a flourishing trade with Asia Minor and the Near East in Leonardo's day.) There were four tapestries on each of the two walls. To attain perspective through his "divine proportion" theory, Leonardo's reduction of the most distant tapestries would have caused them to appear as mere blobs of color, the design lost. Therefore, in order to preserve the natural optical illusion, he subtly distorted the theory. To all appearances, the far tapestries appear in his painting as realistic.

The three-dimensional picture on a flat plane, after all, is older than the *Last Supper* and as modern as Matisse's *Red Studio*.

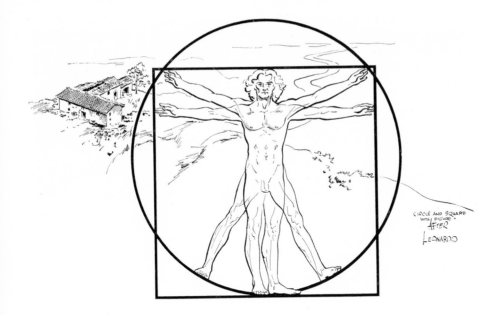

CIRCLE AND SQUARE
WITH FIGURE
AFTER
LEONARDO

Attracted by this similarity in geometrical thought between Leonardo and Matisse, Winter took the time to super-impose a diagram of Matisse-like groupings and lines over a copy of the *Last Supper*. By delineating the invisible lines of direction, he demonstrated that they led to the vanishing point directly behind the central figure of Christ. In all likelihood, Leonardo used his mystical vanishing point as the center of the circle, whose arcs form the pediment just over the head of Christ and, at the opposite side of the circle, the bottom of His robe. The square that is discernible over the circle makes up the geometrical combination Winter recognized in the ancient doorlock of Leonardo's childhood home. The combination is repeated in several places elsewhere in the *Last Supper*.

The central triangle of the painting has been called by some the "spiritual pyramid." The triangle's top is made up of Jesus' portrait, and at its base corners are His hands. The right hand is

91

Photo of original painting in its present condition

said to represent a rejection of temporal power and the left hand implies benevolence and supplication. Christ's right eye is the picture's exact center. The many verticals, horizontals and diagonals throughout the mural reveal Leonardo's further fascination with the Greek idea of "dynamic symmetry."

Winter's explorations of Leonardo's masterpiece were extended as his own reproduction slowly took shape. He learned that Leonardo favored odd numbers within his mathematical theories, particularly the number three. The picture is divided into three areas, the more prominent one being that occupied by the thirteen figures. The other two areas are architectural. There are three windows in the room. The disciples are arranged in four groups of three. In several instances their hands fall into patterns of three.

And yet there were no rules that Winter could pick up and follow for very long. He wondered at times if Leonardo's uses of geometry and mathematics were not frequently subconscious proc-

Photo of Winter's Painting showing application of mathematics

93

esses employed long enough to attain one glorious end, one final effect of magnificence. More than four and a half centuries before, Leonardo had written: "Design is free, in so much as if you see an infinite number of faces they will be all different, one with a long nose and one with a short; the painter therefore must also assume this liberty, and where there is liberty there is no rule."

There were no rules. There was only Leonardo to be rediscovered and explained in his art. And in discovering Leonardo, Winter began to recognize many more recent or contemporary painters. The moderns seemed only to be expounding what Leonardo had originally set forth. The da Vinci stormy sketch showing hell-fire and all the destructive elements being rained on all the universe can be found in several Van Goghs. And the perfect composition of abstract forms may be located in Leonardo's art by diagramming the upper portion of his *Madonna and the Rocks*.

As the outlines of the composition neared completion, Winter began to list those portions missing from the original painting that would require a model. The detail of a foot, a fragment of a face, a bit of drapery would not be guessed at. And, "Be on the watch to take the best parts of many beautiful faces," Leonardo had instructed. Before Winter finished, he had used a living model for at least one part of every face or figure in the *Last Supper*.

The Judas and Christ prototypes as Leonardo rendered them were still the difficult ones to imitate. Winter visited several agencies for professional models in search of a plausible Judas, but to no avail. After one day of futile search, Winter was riding the elevator up to his studio when he noticed the classic profile

Francesco Macedo, who posed for Winter's likeness of Judas

of the Greek-American elevator operator. The man, with the beard of Judas added on, now plays that infamous role in the finished replica.

When some phase of the project would become temporarily snarled, Winter would walk, or sit on a park bench in Union Square. Union Square is one of the few remaining strong-holds of Aristotelian methods of discourse. There is inevitably some person orating to a small group of others. Questions of politics, religion and civil rights are all discussed, argued and preached at almost every hour of the day. Out of habit, Winter began making sketches of the faces that passed by or sat near him. It occurred to him one day that the faces he was sketching possessed the essential qualities he was seeking in models for the disciples. For the professional models had still been found wanting, for the most part. Here in Union Square, he realized, were the faces that showed the same indifference to material considerations that described the apostles. Here were the philosophical attitudes in the heart of a bustling city. Like those of the peripatetic men who had followed Christ about, the faces of Union Square belonged to the world at large.

So three strangers from Union Square posed for Winter. They had no home addresses or telephone numbers. In our day of social categories they would be known as vagrants, perhaps; in the first century they might well have been respected prophets. All of them were familiar with the New Testament and they were moved by the fact that they were representing sainted figures. They came frequently to the studio, even when they were no longer needed, to observe the giant mural take shape. It gladdened them beyond all else, they informed Winter gratefully, that their faces had been chosen to assist in the prolongation of a masterpiece.

96

Detail of Painting showing its deterioration

With one sad exception, the disciples of Christ had been of one mind and purpose. Yet Leonardo painted them as strikingly individualistic and different. He chose difficult and even unnatural poses for them to assume. Winter, principally for that reason, found it necessary to pose a model while he drew so slight a thing as the angle of an eyebrow, a turn of mouth, or a spread of fingers.

The painting of the face of Christ was more troublesome to Winter than Judas had been. A Hebrew friend of his consented to pose for the forehead, nose and mouth, but a face was needed that could portray the noble tranquillity and a wise acceptance of life as it is. It was no more and no less than Leonardo had bequeathed to *his* central figure. Winter found such a face one day.

A man had paused to look into an appliance store window where a television set was being demonstrated. It was a healthy face that rested on the scale of emotions well between the extremes of resignation and fanaticism. Its owner possessed the purposefulness Winter had been desperately looking for. When Winter asked the stranger if he would mind posing for the face of Christ in a painting, the face registered surprise and then joy. He was a Presbyterian minister, Winter later learned.

Leonardo had worried most about hands. Hands, he believed, were one of the essential expressive features of the human body. His delicate craftsmanship was up to fusing his knowledge of anatomy with artistry. A few instances of this survive the ruins of his great painting. One is that the veins on the hands of Christ in the *Last Supper* are more prominent than the veins on the upraised hands of Thomas. Leonardo, who understood the circulatory system long before Harvey (the English doctor generally credited with discovering it), realized that blood drains from an uplifted hand. Raised hands should therefore be paler than those lowered. Winter used the hands of a well-known girl model in working out those of Christ.

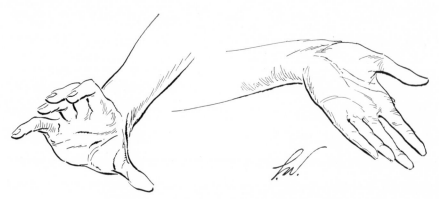

A study for the hands of the central figure

The feet were another matter. A lower strip of the original mural had long been gone. Had Leonardo painted in feet or not? One restorer of the *Last Supper* had inserted them. It was unlikely that a man as insistent upon detail as Leonardo would have left out the feet. Winter included them, taking his cue as to the sandal styles and foot positions from Marco d'Oggionno, one of Leonardo's apprentices who later made a copy of his master's *Last Supper*. Another model posed for the feet of Jesus which Winter proportioned to the hands, although not delicately enough to leave an impression that the divine figure was effeminate. The feet of John held up Winter again. In what position should they be painted? They might have appeared under the table in a hundred places and in a hundred ways. Finally, a choice was made.

There was even time to dwell upon the aged rumor that Leonardo had painted Thaddeus while looking at his own face in a mirror. It has also been suggested that Christ might have been, in part, a self-portrait by Leonardo. There is certainly a likeness among the two figures of Christ and Thomas and the self-portrait of Leonardo. It is possible that Leonardo might have posed for some part of Christ's face or for Thaddeus, but not both men, Winter decided. Leonardo never would have permitted one model to serve for two subjects.

When the composition was traced in red chalk, Winter and his helpers carefully laid out the outlines by brush. He depended upon the colors to extend the illusion of depth perception. Color was also the best way he found to emphasize those points of the picture Leonardo had stressed. One head could be made to stand out over another by an adroit application of paint. Looking directly into the picture, one sensed the invisible vertical planes that separated the forestage from the middlestage, and the middlestage from the background. These divisions could only be atmospherically suggested through color, shadings and tones. Years after Leonardo, Puvis de Chavannes maintained soft grays and indistinct shades by keeping a screen of cheese cloth between himself and his models. Leonardo had merely waited for an early or late Italian sun to provide him with the same tonal relationships.

Before finishing his re-creation, Winter used nearly three hundred dollars' worth of fine English colors. They were permanent colors containing no dyes or vegetable matters. The texture of these earth colors, made from finely ground pigment of clay or rock, has not changed much since the Renaissance days. Leonardo would have used all the earth colors including lapis which is made from blue Italian stone. The color was popular in the master's day but its supply is almost exhausted today. Winter believed that Leonardo, who respected Montorfano as a decorator, would have painted with the Venetian and Naples yellows that Montorfano used in the *Crucifixion,* opposite the *Last Supper.* Winter mixed special yellows to match the tones of Montorfano's, recorded on Winter's color notes. He also knew that there were no oxides in Leonardo's paints, and these facts were important to his effort at reproducing the *Last Supper* colors as they had once been before the years of dirt and decay had modified them. It is difficult to remember, viewing the *Last Supper* in Milan today, that Leonardo's hues once ran the tonal scale from light to dark. Now the windows in the banquet room are only light by their contrast with the surrounding darkened composition.

Work in Winter's studio went on simultaneously on the scaffolding and at the floor level. The painting fell into two general divisions: the underpainting which would set the general tone for the middlestage and background areas of the picture, and the overpainting. The overpainting was concerned with colors and light and shade relationships. Finally, there would be glazing with a tool to obtain the final texture of the mural's surface.

Underpainting had been popular in the Early Renaissance before Leonardo's time. Unlike the nineteenth-century artists who painted what they saw directly on the canvas in a single layer of colors, the old masters made use of the transparent properties of paint. Like Leonardo, they established construction and form by applying several layers of paint on their panels. This was working from the inside out instead of the more modern reversed way of doing it. Leonardo spent a great portion of his time in modeling the substructure of a painting. His underpainting was usually a brown monochrome, and this explains the dark effect of his backgrounds, since no matter how light or transparent a layer of color happened to be that he put over the previous coat, it still darkened the tone.

Where Leonardo brought on something of a revolution in technique was in his use of chiaroscuro, the creation of atmosphere and unity of form through the manipulations of light and shade. The study of color, light and shade monopolizes dozens of pages of Leonardo's notebooks. Primitive painters like Sassetta, and the Early Renaissance masters like Botticelli, had brought out their backgrounds as sharply as their foregrounds. But Leonardo subtly pointed up what he wished to be the high-lights of his work. The heads of Christ and Thomas are conspicuous in the *Last Supper,* less because of emphasis given directly to those heads by Leonardo, than that they are silhouetted against the windows, lit by the setting sun. The head of Christ, in fact, is the point of strongest contrast: the darkest dark of His figure against the lightest light of the window. All such contrasts taken together give the impression of a third dimension. The warm colors indoors are always miles away from the cool blue of the mountains in the distance. "Black will seem most intense when it is against a background of greater whiteness," Leonardo wrote in one of his typical over-simplifications.

Leonardo would frequently apply paint with his hands, molding the color with his fingers into the surface effects he wished. One result of such glazing was an impression similar to that received from today's colored slides of photographs when they are shown against frosted glass. The light of the modern projector goes through the translucent slide, strikes the frosted glass and returns, showing up the colors of the slide and giving the picture a quality of three dimensions. X-ray photographs of Renaissance art reveal that glazes of transparent colors were used frequently on the purest of white gesso ground. The theory here was that outside light would penetrate the layers of color, strike the white undercoating of the picture and reflect back, colored on the return trip by the thin painted layers through which the light must travel. The glazed, uneven surface of the picture would diffuse and transform these reflected colors, rendering them less obvious and more natural to the eye. "The surface of every opaque body," wrote Leonardo, "will participate in the color of the bodies placed against it."

While a modern artist like Van Gogh worked essentially in color, and a painter like Albert Ryder, in tone, Leonardo was careful to emphasize one technique or picture area over others only where their cumulative effects were sure to add up to a picture story of dramatic unity and aesthetic balance. His color scheme in the *Last Supper* was composed of the three primaries: red, blue, and yellow. The red and blue were juxtaposed on Christ's figure to create the full emotional impact. The subordinate characters were dressed in more subtle shades. To reproduce these original achievements in color, Winter was given one conspicuous advantage over Leonardo: working on canvas, Winter was able to alter his colors to his final satisfaction. When Leonardo transferred his preliminary work to the wet plaster wall, he could only have had time for a hasty change or two before the colors had dried into the plaster.

Casual sketch of Paris rooftops from Montemartre during Winter's stay in Paris

Monument of Leonardo on the public square in Milan

CHAPTER VII

The Exhibition

WHEN THE re-creation of the *Last Supper* was finished in late 1951, the enormous canvas was unveiled at the Architectural League in New York City. Winter was prepared for rough treatment at the hands of the art critics but there was none forthcoming. Tolstoy, in an essay discussing art and art criticism once wrote: "Most people are infected by the artist's feeling and his work becomes known. Then criticism, discussing the artist, says that the work is not bad, but all the same the artist is not a Dante, nor a Shakespeare, nor a Goethe, nor a Raphael, nor what Beethoven was in his last period."

Winter sat in one corner of the exhibit room during the showing, on hand to answer questions or to receive comment.

This reproduction, the critics straightaway informed Winter, was not bad. It was, in fact, good. It showed an enormous amount of fine work. But surely, while no living man could say just what the original da Vinci had been like, and this was no doubt as accurate an approximation to the Milan mural that could be accomplished, Mr. Winter, it must be admitted, was not Leonardo.

This, of course, was quite true, replied Winter. After all, he

105

had been born in Illinois and an artist from Illinois would not paint just the way an artist from Vinci painted five hundred years ago. Something American must be in the painting somewhere, although his most conscientious efforts had been channelled toward painting the picture as Leonardo-like as possible. After all, Winter went on, he had loved what he had painted in the *Last Supper* and no artist can leave himself completely out of so subjective a situation. One could only hope and believe that one had conveyed in some significant measure an expression of the original message and meaning, could one not?

The editor of the *American Artist* magazine and the art editor of the *American Weekly* found the work worthy of reproduction in their periodicals. Others retained pre-conceived contentions that greatness can never be imitated satisfactorily.

Those who gave Winter his greatest reward were those who came to the League building to reap a spiritual harvest rather than to form artistic evaluations. There were the service chaplains and regular clergymen who spent as much as a half day before the painting. Usually they would explain to Winter that they had never seen the original *Last Supper,* and that prospects of their doing so were remote. Mr. Winter would therefore understand their gratitude to him and Mr. Holton for this re-creation and faithful copy of a famous work. A man's religion is within his heart and soul, to be sure, but it was a joyous thing, these men of the cloth told Winter, to see a pictorial reflection of one's faith. A joyous thing, indeed.

Then there were the Catholics who genuflexed and said the rosary before the painted figures of Christ and the disciples. There were the curious who sat in chairs and stared in silent wonderment. There were the ladies who always came alone and would sit out the hour before the canvas, some with tears, some with serenity. Winter wondered who they were and just what they were finding in his painting. What drama were they living out? What particular hunger could such a picture satiate or even aggravate? But it didn't matter after a few days of watching the spectators whether a critic praised the painting or whether he found something to fuss over.

To those who had seen Leonardo's subdued original mural, or a fair reprint of it, Winter's painting, done as it was in the high key that Leonardo is thought to have painted in, was at first startling, with its pronounced, shimmering colors. Lionello Venturi, a contemporary art connoisseur, recently remarked:

> It is significant, and perhaps saddening, to see how the youthful, carefree joy of the Renaissance has already vanished in even Leonardo's earliest works. Bright colors have given place to somber tones; clean-cut outlines to blurred lines that merge forms in an all-pervading dusk; the sunny morning light to the sadness of that dim hour when day is dying and night has not yet fallen. The crowd in *The Adoration of the Magi* is haunted by strange fears, in agonized suspense; its joy has changed to panic, as if some cataclysm were impending. And it was not without good reason that Pater read into La Gioconda's smile the sad, accumulated experience of untold ages of human sufferings and sins.

The *Last Supper* was claimed by Holton after its New York showing. Following a short tour during which he showed the work to various church groups, Holton had the painting hung in the Holton Museum on Biscayne Boulevard in Miami, Florida. The building had been built by him expressly for housing the repro-

107

duction, and the gallery where it is now on exhibition is dimensionally the same as the Milan refectory, except for a shorter wall height. Winter, who under-painted and glazed the canvas six times, retained the right to make any changes in the painting that he might later deem advisable. An artist's age-old grievance, after all, is that by the nature of his profession he must be separated from his creations almost as soon as he has completed them and is left with only photographs, sketches or reprints of the work to serve as evidence of those joys and periods of distress that marked their accomplishments.

One print of Winter's *Last Supper* was sent to Vinci, Italy. The village's mayor, Guido Masi, wrote to the artist:

> Like me, all the citizens of Vinci and everyone in the world who admires the genius, Leonardo da Vinci, should hold you in high esteem for having assured our descendants in a more indestructible manner the vision of that which is the greatest work of art of all times.
> We Vincians must particularly thank you for reviving the memory of the surroundings of the childhood and youth of Leonardo which contributed decisively to his spiritual formation.

The extent of failure or success of Winter's unusual commission may not be determined for decades. Winter believes that time will lend the work some of that mystical and spiritual quality which finally came to rest with Leonardo's masterpiece. And under normal conditions of art custodianship, the re-creation should survive for two thousand more years.

*Drawing of sculpture by La Monaca on Leonardo's tomb
at Amboise, France.*

FOUR SKETCHES

Ruins of the room where Leonardo was born.

Col. Vinci, May 8 51

Old oven in Casa Leonardo
Vinci, May 18 '51

A part of Casa Leonardo
Vinci, May 1851

Paris, Mäy 11 51

Model used by Winter for the figure of Christ in The Last Supper

Crucifixion (*oil*) *by Lumen Winter*